MEMPHIS BLUES BARBEQUE HOUSE

MEMPHIS BLUES BARBEQUE HOUSE

BRINGIN' SOUTHERN BBQ HOME

by George Siu and Park Heffelfinger

whitecap

Whitecap Books is known for its expertise in the cookbook market, and has produced some of the most innovative and familiar titles found in kitchens across North America.

Edited by Nadine Boyd
Proofread by Joan Tetrault
Design by Michelle Mayne
Photography by Chris Mason Stearns
Photography on pages 19 and 22–27 by David Denyer

Printed in Canada by Friesens

Library and Archives Canada Cataloguing in Publication

Siu, George

     Memphis Blues Barbeque House : bringin' southern BBQ home / George Siu, Park Heffelfinger.

Includes index.

ISBN 978-1-55285-914-8

     1. Barbecue cookery. I. Heffelfinger, Park II. Title.

TX840.B3S558 2008   641.5′784   C2007-905568-0

The publisher acknowledges the financial support of the Government of Canada through the Book Publishing Industry Development Program (BPIDP) and the Province of British Columbia through the Book Publishing Tax Credit.

First, we dedicate this book to our families, who stuck with us through many long nights and weekends.

Secondly, we dedicate this book to our other family—the core group of hard-working staff without whom none of this would have been possible.

Finally, we dedicate this book to all of our loyal customers who keep coming back over the years.

Contents

Foreword

I've always had an affinity for slow-cooked foods. Stews, braises, and baked beans from my grandmother's kitchen; confit, cassoulet, and tagines that I discovered as a young cook; and now, as a chef, experimenting with *sous-vide*, a technique involving vacuum packs in a water circulator set at a very precise, low heat—a technique becoming more and more popular in the kitchens of high-end restaurants. No matter how simple or how complicated, there's no denying that slow cooking has a way of intensifying flavor.

And then there's barbecue. I *love* barbecue. And I am not referring to a piece of fancy beef tenderloin slapped over a gas flame and then doused with sugary sauce from a bottle. I'm talking *real* barbecue—where the best and tastiest cuts of meat are rubbed with a tried-and-true blend of spices, and then slowly cooked for hours with natural wood, allowing distinctive smoky flavors to be infused throughout the juicy meat.

This is the kind of barbecue you get at Memphis Blues Barbeque House, and the kind of barbecue you'll find in this book. George and Park make a conscious decision to do barbecue right every day—they don't take shortcuts. They put all of their passion and energy into their recipes by investing in the proper equipment, and applying proven techniques to the highest quality ingredients. The two have created the type of restaurant that I not only enjoy, but that I also truly believe in supporting: Simple. Honest. Well executed.

Barbecue is a technique I have yet to master, and so I'm looking forward to experimenting with the secrets that the boys are about to share with us here. This is a book you can't do without if you enjoy cooking and if you love *real* barbecue.

George and Park—thanks for bringing us a little Southern warmth to the cold dark north.

Robert Clark
Executive Chef of C Restaurant,
Nu Restaurant, and Raincity Grill

Introduction

GEORGE ON FOOD

I've always loved food . . . all kinds of food. My nanny was an incredible cook and my love of food started as soon as I was fed solids. I used to watch her cook up a storm every night when I was growing up—the smells were incredible. Pan-fried garlic and ginger beef, braised duck with taro root, and giant wok-seared prawns; this little woman could put together a six-dish dinner better than anyone I know.

Growing up Chinese, and especially in my family, I had to eat everything! If I dared leave a morsel on my plate, my father would glare me down until I finished it. I remember being in Hong Kong when I was very young and eating barbecued pigeon, satay, and cold noodle dishes at a barbecue where nearly everything was cooked on hibachis. I guess you could call it my first barbecue epiphany.

When I travel abroad, I always eat what the locals eat. Nothing says "I love your culture" more than devouring a plate of local cuisine. I've had great meals in New York, Barcelona, Paris, Rome, Hong Kong, and Vancouver. High-end or lowbrow, it's been a delicious gastronomic journey. I went through a phase where I ate a lot of foie gras, truffles, and foods that were stacked in towers. But you know what? My love is for simple food done well. There's something soulful about a bowl of chicken congee on a cold morning or a Sunday dinner of prime rib and Yorkshire pudding drowning in gravy.

Being such a lover of food I naturally wanted to learn to be a good cook. I was a teenager (in the late '80s) when I had the pleasure of working with a chef from London. His name was Alan Dunelle and I learned an incredible amount from him. He taught me the basics of French cooking—but the best lesson he taught me was to trust my instincts and feel my food.

In Alan's world there were only two types of cooks: the technical cook and the intuitive cook. I guess I've always been an intuitive cook, but he really helped me

is to jot down a lot of notes about the likable characteristics of pleasing varieties grown in certain climates. Wine is one of the great pleasures in life and one I definitely plan on enjoying until my last days.

I began taking more advanced classes and at one of these courses I met Park. We quickly developed a friendship through the love of good food and wine. We would get together often to cook, drink, and exchange food stories. At times, we would talk about the next great food concept.

Barbecue has always been one of my favorite ways of cooking. I find the smells intoxicating and the cleanup easy. I remember my dad barbecuing T-bone steaks and wieners on a Weber charcoal grill when we were growing up. It was tough to control the heat and the flare-ups on that grill, so we always had charred food (not to mention the flavor from the starter fluid and cheap charcoal).

I started cooking on a hibachi when I moved out. I cooked a lot of satays on that little grill and quickly learned how to control the heat and flare-ups. I would have a pair of tongs and a can nearby for dropping pieces of hot charcoal into. I would either remove charcoal from the grill and place it in the can or take the hot charcoal from the can to maintain proper heat and to control flare-ups. I was king of the satay because of this little trick.

I began experimenting with marinades on different cuts of meat. For me, pork was the meat of choice. Beef, chicken, seafood, and vegetables were good but pork was great. I could dry-rub it, marinate it, sauce it on the grill, or even add wood chips to the

flourish. I started cooking on the line at a large restaurant chain even though I was part of the front house management team. I really enjoyed the pace, the organization, the rush of being slammed, and the satisfaction of completing 300 orders.

As for wine, my first experience was with a bottle of Blue Nun. What god-awful stuff. I was 15 and hanging out with the boys down at the creek. I became ill and vomited all over the place (but that's for another book). And by 16 I was a connoisseur, having moved on to Black Tower, Mateus, Blue Danube, and Hochtaler.

I started taking wine seriously in my twenties. I took beginner wine courses and learned to look at the colors, smells, and tastes of different varieties. I became interested in the growing, production, and marketing of wine and the ever-changing wine landscape. I educated myself with wine books and attended as many wine tastings as I could. I think the key to knowing your taste in wine charcoal for a little smokiness. Cooking with charcoal added that extra flavor that you can't get on a gas grill (unless you're a food geek like me who will experiment on one until you get it right). So I bought a gas grill out of convenience.

Of course, I grilled a lot when I first got my gas grill, but I missed that smoky flavor I was getting from my hibachi. I started smoking ribs using a smoker box over indirect heat. A 2.5 lb (1.25 kg) slab of side ribs would take about three hours at 300°F (150°C), and I would reload the smoker box two or three times. The ribs turned out fantastic and sometimes I would turn on the burner directly under the ribs and do a mop with sauce to finish them off.

One of my favorite things to cook this way was Cornish hen. It would barbecue up juicy and plump. I made a lot of different rubs when I barbecued this way: a milder rub for chicken, hens, and ribs, and a spicier rub for beef and lamb to match their stronger flavors. For me though, pulled pork was the real deal, but I just couldn't get it right on a gas grill. So I decided I would build a barbecue pit in my backyard.

I enlisted the help of a good friend, Tim Nye, to assist me in building my barbecue pit. We looked at different designs and eventually settled on one we thought could hold up in Vancouver rain. It was more like a brick oven (*forno*). We built it next to my patio, and let me tell you, it was backbreaking work.

We dug a hole that was 3 feet wide, 5 feet long, and 2 feet deep for the foundation. We filled the hole with crushed rocks and gravel.

We used retaining wall bricks that interlock so we could build on a solid foundation. We built it up about 4½ feet so I wouldn't have to crouch when I was using the oven. It took at least four trips to the gardening store before we had enough bricks—I think I killed the back shocks on my Grand Am hauling them. I remember driving down Lougheed Highway with my tail pipe scraping the pavement.

Next, we filled the center cavity of the foundation with more crushed rocks and gravel and leveled it with paving slabs. Then we layered firebricks on the pavers to create the cooking surface. We used a 45-gallon cardboard drum cut in half as the mold for the top. We wrapped the drum with chicken wire so the cement mixture would stick.

The cement was made from a combination of sand, clay, cement, and water. Tim would shovel it onto the chicken-wired cardboard drum and I would smooth it out. We cut a 4-inch (10 cm) hole near the front of the oven so we could insert a 4-foot galvanized duct to act as the chimney. We built a door that would fit over it so I could control the airflow; it was an opening where I could put food in, take food out, and feed the oven with wood.

That mixture was a pain to get right—too much water and it wouldn't hold up, too much cement and the oven would crumble from the heat. Finally, after two long days we were done. We wrapped it with burlap sacks and kept it damp for a week to help cure the cement.

Finally it was ready to be fired up. I pulled out as much of the cardboard drum as

I could reach, but there was a big piece left. I couldn't reach it so I picked up my daughter, who was four at the time, and put her in the oven so she could get it. There I was holding her feet, the only part of her sticking out of the oven. Thank God my neighbor didn't call child services.

Still, there were pieces of the cardboard drum left, so I loaded the oven up with wood and fired her up. I let it burn for a couple of hours; it cracked a little, which is to be expected, but it held together. There was a lot of smoke coming from the oven and my neighbors and fire department all paid me a visit. I thought I'd have to shut 'er down because I didn't have a permit for this thing. But it turned out they were all into barbecue. For the next couple of weeks people brought me apple and cherry wood.

I started cooking pizzas and bread on the firebricks and they all had a smoky flavor to them. But the reason I built this thing was to make great barbecue. I used some seasoned black walnut for my first smoking. I smoked a pork roast with a simple black pepper, garlic, salt, and paprika rub. It was a bit on the dry side because I had yet to master the heat within the oven, but it had a good smoke flavor and a nice crust.

After I realized how well the oven kept the heat, I would burn off logs to get the oven up to temperature, then take most of them out, leaving enough hot coals to lay some apple wood on. I would put in whatever meat I was smoking in a cast-iron pan and close the door. Then I would open the door, wrap the meat in tinfoil, and add more logs to finish it off. If I wanted to sauce it, I would remove the tinfoil, brush on the sauce, and let the meat finish off in the oven. Soon, I was barbecuing ribs, chicken, lamb, sausages, and beef. Pulled pork, it turned out, was another matter.

I knew Park had a water smoker and we decided to get together and make pulled pork. We started with a small 6 lb (2.7 kg) pork shoulder, dry-rubbed it, and smoked it in the water smoker for about four hours. We then put it into the wood oven with apple wood smoke for another two hours and wrapped it in tinfoil for the final hour in the oven. It was magic! It was moist, smoky, and delicious. We made a sweet tomato barbecue sauce and piled it high on a bun—our first pulled pork sandwich of many. We started having barbecue parties at my place and invited friends over to try the 'cue as we worked to perfect it.

My culinary history is mostly self-taught—I just enjoy being in a busy kitchen. I'm always learning about food and how many different ways you can make a dish. For me, the best part about being in this business is creating dishes my clients will enjoy. The satisfaction is that they keep coming back. The topper? I can be myself while doing it.

I think Memphis Blues Barbeque House has become a success through our love of food, but especially our love of barbecue.

PARK'S STORY

When I was a little boy, my mother did most of the cooking on a day-to-day basis, but on weekends (especially Sundays) the kitchen was my father's domain. On Sunday mornings we used to get kippered herring with scrambled eggs, or a concoction he called Eggs Parmesan (eggs baked with Parmesan cheese and dry sherry). It was pretty sophisticated for Winnipeg in the '50s.

My father had the complete series of the Time Life Foods of the World cookbooks. He would frequently use them as a resource for his gourmet Sunday night supper (to be enjoyed in front of the Ed Sullivan Show). As a child, I loved to pore over those books. I dreamed of the exotic creations that graced the pages. In my teens I picked up a complete set of 24 at a yard sale for $1 each. I guess I was destined to be a foodie.

My first job in a restaurant was at a small burger joint in Goderich, Ontario. We sold bait, fishing tackle, breakfast, and burgers. When I graduated from university, I decided to try a stint in the fine dining business. That experiment turned out to be a disaster—I was fired after six months for badmouthing the owner (who happened to be standing behind me) to the other staff.

Tail between my legs, I went back to school and got a diploma in hospitality man-

agement. After several jobs in hotels and restaurants in England and Sweden, I landed a junior management position at Bridges restaurant in Vancouver, BC. That period opened me up to the possibilities of food and wine as a way of life.

I revisited my Time Life Foods of the World series and learned about regional French cooking and the concept of fresh local food, and I even attempted my first cassoulet. Later, I met some amazing people who sparked my interest in wine, including my friend Richard Harvey. He inspired me to study, so I traveled again to Europe to attend the British Wine and Spirits Education Trust. With this knowledge under my belt, I returned to Canada and got a great job as a sommelier at a small Toronto eatery called Le Select Bistro.

In the late '80s, I returned to Vancouver to get into the wine retail business. I also started a wine education company called The Vancouver Wine Academy with partner Mark Davidson. After ten years of retail and wine education, the restaurant business found me again—I've noticed that life often comes full circle.

Barbecue was one of those things that I fell into by circumstance. First of all, I am obsessed with food; I have always played around in both home and restaurant kitchens. I love all things related to food.

In 1998, George and I were returning from a business trip in New Orleans, and we had a stopover in the Memphis airport. Walking through the airport to our next gate, our noses led us to a very busy takeout window at Jim Neely's Interstate Barbecue. Our mouths were watering as the workers chopped fresh pulled pork and piled it onto enormous buns with slaw and beautiful mahogany sauce. We were grinning like kids in a candy store.

We snuck our pulled pork sandwiches onto the plane and smirked at our wives. We carefully opened the brown paper bags of pulled pork goodness and the smells instantly wafted throughout the plane. Passengers began murmuring questions like, "Are we getting a meal on this flight?" We weren't. Call buttons were pushed to ask the busy flight attendants, "When's dinner and what is that smell?" We shared bite after luscious bite of our dripping sandwiches with our wives, and I knew right then that there was no turning back. I was hooked. That's my story and I'm sticking to it.

Around that same time, I visited my brother, Totton, in Toronto. He had a home water smoker and had gotten heavily into barbecue independently of me. He hooked me up with my own water smoker, which I shipped back to Vancouver (unavailable in British Columbia at the time). By that time, Tot had perfected quite a few recipes and he shared his sauces and dry rubs with me. Back in Vancouver, I tried to duplicate that fabulous pulled pork sandwich I had shared with George that fateful day at the Memphis airport. Using Totton's tips, I got close to replicating Memphis-style pulled pork, but it took a research trip to the South to really fine-tune the recipes. Tot is still into barbecue and over the years we have swapped recipes and techniques. Some of his rubs and sauces appear in the following pages.

George was also inspired by our Memphis experience, and was building a backyard brick oven at his home in suburban Vancouver. For the next year, George and I talked barbecue, ate barbecue, and cooked barbecue. We shared our bounty with friends and family, who kept encouraging us In the fall of 2000, our friend Bennet simply said, "You guys should open a restaurant." Up until that time, we had been pursuing different careers; I was in the wine business and George was in real estate development. George and I looked at each other and shrugged. There was no reason not to. We had to do it.

In short, we wrote a business plan and submitted it to three banks. Lo and behold, we were offered the seed money, and after putting our houses up for collateral, we had the money for our first location. The rest is history.

MEMPHIS IN MAY

In 2001, once Park and I had written our business plan for Memphis Blues, and our goals were coming to fruition, we had a few weeks of free time. We headed down to Memphis, Tennessee, for further research. Tennessee is the land of Elvis and barbecue. The Memphis in May World Championship Barbecue Cooking Contest was in full swing when we arrived. For this one week each May, Memphis is home to hundreds of competing teams—they come from all over the world. A ridiculous amount of money and bragging rights are awarded to the Grand Champion, and the winner of each category also acquires money and awards. There are categories for best ribs, best butt (pulled or chopped pork), best beef brisket, best chicken, and even best display. Some teams build a functional replica of their restaurant or a famous landmark to represent where they're from. There were over 50,000 people visiting for this competition. It was exhausting and exhilarating. We spent two weeks doing industrial espionage. We tasted tons of barbecue. Some of it was good, some of it was great.

The city was packed with barbecue competitors and media. We tried to book a room late and there were no rooms available. We finally found a place on the east side of Memphis. All we knew was that it was a rooming house owned by a guy named James. We were ready for the adventure to begin.

When we got to the house James was there to greet us and showed us to our room. The room was 10 by 12 feet and had three bunk beds ... not exactly what we had in

mind. We looked at each other, swore under our breath, and then conceded by saying, "Hey, we're here, so let's make the best of it."

We were definitely there to experience Memphis in May, but we were also there for the barbecue in the city. We ate barbecue for every meal the next week. Each morning we would map out where we wanted to eat and always asked our cab drivers about their favorite places. The first night our cabbie took us to the Rendezvous Restaurant—a restaurant that seats over 200 people—for a taste of Memphis-style ribs. At the Rendezvous, we decided to check out the pit area as we were being seated. They had two cooking areas and a kitchen that put out side dishes and nonbarbecue items. There were four cooks at each station and they were hustling. The pits were made of bricks with heavy cast-iron doors. As they opened the doors we could see racks and racks of ribs smoking and cooking away.

You can have ribs two ways at the Rendezvous: wet or dry. We ordered one of each with beans, cornbread, slaw, and sauce. Dry ribs come right out of the pit with dry rub seasoning sprinkled on the meat, and the sauce is served on the side. Wet ribs come out of the pit and are finished on the char grill. Barbecue sauce is mopped on the meat in the last few minutes of grilling. The mop caramelizes and results in messy, saucy ribs. The dry ribs were our favorite. One of the cooks told us the Rendezvous goes through four tons of ribs per week.

Tops Barbecue was next on our list. There are two or three locations and they look like every other fast food outlet in town. We walked in, told them we were researching Memphis-style barbecue, and they took us into their kitchen. The pit master was a gentleman in his fifties who had been working at that location since it opened. He had a brick barbecue pit built into the building

and it had a black steel door. When he fed charcoal into the fire pit, we saw three racks of pork shoulders cooking overtop of the charcoal. It was so hot in there we were sweating just watching him sweat. He had a hose handy in case he wanted to cool the coals down and control the heat in the pit. The pulled pork sandwiches were fantastic. They were served on white burger buns with slaw on the bottom and a sweet tomato-based sauce on top.

Once James saw how passionate we were about barbecue, he decided to take us to one of his favorite places for 'cue, the Cozy Corner. It was a building in a bad part of town that looked like any other fast food restaurant. The first thing we noticed after walking

in was that the walls were covered with photos of blues masters and actors. B.B. King, John Lee Hooker, and Muddy Waters peered down at us. There was even a picture of Cybil Shepherd with the owner. But the one picture that stopped us in our tracks was Julia Child. What in the world was Julia Child doing in a

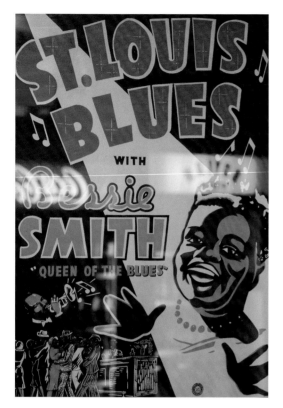

barbecue joint in Memphis? The owner told us she came for the Cornish hens—they were her favorite. We knew right then that James had brought us to one of those great joints that only locals know about. We ordered ribs, pulled pork sandwiches, barbecued bologna, brisket . . . and the Cornish game hen, of course.

In the kitchen, they had a pit made of brick and glass. The entire cooking area was made from heat-tempered glass. You could see the racks and all the meat on them as they were being barbecued. The owner thought it was cool for people to see their food cooking. It was.

The pork was tender, smoky, and delicious. Like at Tops Barbecue, it was served on a white hamburger bun with slaw and a sweet, red barbecue sauce. I asked why the generic white bun and James's reply was simple: "It's not about the bun, it's all about the pork." The ribs were smoky and tasty, served dry with sauce on the side. I did the rib test by pulling them apart to see how well they were cooked. The meat split between the bone and not off the bone. They had a pink smoke ring and a nice mahogany color to them. Cooked to perfection. The bologna . . . well, it didn't do it for us. It was a loaf of bologna thrown in the pit and smoked for a few hours.

They offered an unusual item: barbecued spaghetti. They mixed cooked spaghetti with barbecue sauce and bits of burnt meat ends, and finished it off in the smoker for a couple of hours. Tasty, but too much barbecue sauce for our liking.

I have to mention that James owned a brand new white Cadillac. We were being driven around Memphis going from one barbecue joint to the next. I'm sure we looked out of place in this pristine Caddie at some of these establishments—especially this next place.

James thought a trip to the rougher part of town for some soul food was in order. We drove for a couple of miles into a neighborhood that looked like a war zone. Abandoned, dilapidated buildings towered over the sidewalks and gutted cars on blocks littered the streets. "We're not in Kansas anymore, Dorothy," I said.

We finally pulled up to a corner store with wire cages on the windows and steel bars riveted into the front door. The building was dirty, and an illegible sign was hanging off one hinge. There was a barrel to one side of the door that looked like it was used for fires, and a group of men loitering by the front. They were staring hard and the looks on their faces were priceless. It was a mixture of "Are you kiddin' me?" and "Are you boys lost?"

I was sitting in the back seat trying to not make eye contact when Park and James both turned and told me to go in. "Not to worry," they said. They would wait in the car. "Screw you guys," was my reply. James explained that this was the place for soul food and good ribs—so I relented, and went in.

As I got out I heard the doors lock behind me and James kept the car running. I was committed at this point. I entered the store and noticed about five customers all hanging by the cash counter and chatting. Everybody stopped when they saw me standing by the door. You could hear a cockroach crawl across the counter. I declared: "I'm here to eat soul food and 'cue 'cause I hear it's the best around."

Suddenly, smiles appeared and the chatter began again. They welcomed me like a long-lost brother. Two of the guys showed me to the hot table at the back of the store. Man, that place smelled good. There were grits, cheese grits, cornbread, collard greens, ham hocks with black-eyed peas, fried chicken, catfish, pig's tails, chitlins, pecan pie, sweet potato pie, red velvet cake, and candied yams. I beckoned to the men in the car to come inside. After four hours, late into the afternoon, there was no barbecue left.

Even though I had eaten three meals during our stay, I placed a good-sized takeout order. Since there was no more barbecue,

I ordered a few soul food items: ham hocks with black-eyed peas, collard greens, cornbread, and sweet potato pie. Food, it seems, can cross cultural boundaries better than diplomacy.

Next up was the Commissary in Germantown, a suburb of Memphis. The building looked like it was built around the turn of the century, and it had what must have been a hundred-year old oak tree in the front. You can literally smell the smoky barbecue from a mile away. The smell has permeated the floorboards, ceilings, walls, and even the washrooms. Most of the service staff looked like they'd been there since the house was built.

We had to find another gear when the food came: this was going to be our fifth meal of the day. We stretched ourselves appropriately. The ribs were outstanding—tender and smoky with a defined smoke ring—falling off the bone, but with chew. The generous

portion of pulled pork was also tasty and tender. The sides were excellent: mustardy potato salad, creamy slaw, and smoky sweet beans. The cornbread was cake-like and served with butter and honey. We both liked it.

When we told the pit master, a gentleman in his late fifties who loved his work, that we were on a quest for the greatest 'cue experience known to mankind, he showed us to the pit. It was made of brick and built into the kitchen wall. It had a steel door and when he opened it you could see five racks of ribs, chickens, and sausages being barbecued. We asked him about cooking times and he said the ribs take about four to four and a half hours, the chickens about three hours, and the sausages about one hour. He checks on everything with his meat fork. Sometimes he pulls the ribs early because "some folks like more chew." According to this pit master, you should never serve sauce on your ribs because "you must be hiding something if you gotta have sauce on them." Sauce should always be served on the side. He comes in at 3:00 a.m. to smoke the pork butts so they are ready when they open. He was cooking with charcoal and smoking with hickory.

The Memphis in May competition takes place along the banks of the Mississippi. It was hot and muggy; the smell of wood smoke and barbecued meat wafted through the fairgrounds. We didn't know a soul. Hundreds of teams toiled away at their various tasks, and fence barriers kept the crowds of gawkers out. Actually, we think it was to keep the other teams out. Barbecue competition is a world cloaked in secret ingredients, sauces, and rubs—everyone's looking for an edge. We were a bit naive thinking we could just waltz in and hang out with the team of our choice.

We started schmoozing as many teams as possible so we could get invited into their inner circle. (Of course, they would have to

share their secrets with us if we were invited in, right?) Most teams didn't give us the time of day and others thought we were a bit odd. It didn't help that we were filming everything and everybody with a camcorder. Meanwhile, Park was asking questions about barbecue and taking notes on his little note pad. Looking back, I'm sure they thought we were spying for another team.

Needless to say, with the unwelcoming reception, we planned our departure from the festivities. Before we called it a day, however, we thought we'd talk to one last team. They were the Southern Gentlemen's Culinary Society. They all looked like members of ZZ Top, and were drinking beer and Jack Daniel's. Park did most of the talking because he could almost pass for one of their cousins.

It turned out they had been watching us and had no problem with us hanging out with them during the competition. One of the fellows, Archie, took one look at us and figured we were from north of the Mason-Dixon Line (and therefore represented no threat to him or his trade secrets). Archie had a brother-in-law on the team, Mike. Mike's nickname was Sarge. Why? We could only guess. It could be that he resembled a saber-wielding Confederate soldier. He did rule the roost with a heavy hand.

After brief introductions they offered us a beer. They owned a restaurant in Little Rock, Arkansas, called the Whole Hog Cafe—their restaurant is filled with trophies they've won over the years. They've competed every year in the Memphis in May competition. They showed us their tricked-

out Airstream trailer complete with bourbon bar and air conditioning, which they used when the judges visited.

They were competing in two categories that year: Best Ribs and the Whole Hog. Archie was sure this was going to be their year, so he bought a 125 lb (56 kg) Berkshire hog from Manitoba, Canada. To barbecue this hog and compete in this category, Sarge and Archie built a 5-foot-long by 4-foot-high metal box. It looked like a coffin! The bottom section was filled with charcoal and there was a panel through which they could remove the ashes or add more charcoal. There was a second panel that could be removed so they could add wood onto the charcoal. The top opened so the pig could be laid onto a wire grill. There was a thermometer to keep track of the internal temperature and the flue had a damper on it to monitor the amount of smoke and heat inside.

It took more than 24 hours to cook the hog—it had to be spritzed with an apple juice rub every hour. The team took turns napping in their trailer (no one really sleeps at these events).

While the hog was doing its thing in the smoker, we started asking questions about the team's history and cooking techniques. We inquired about what to look for when buying a pit and cuts of meat and trims. They were passionate about what they were doing, and they shared a lot of knowledge. They thought the best way to learn was to apply the lesson immediately, so Sarge and Archie promptly put us to work. (Being the entrepreneurs they are, they also had a pit and trailer at the concession to sell barbecue to the public.)

We were assigned removal of the membrane from the backside of the ribs. This helps the ribs cook evenly and allows the smoke to penetrate the rack. After that we were off to trim briskets before dry-rubbing them for the pit. At this point Archie gave us a lesson on rubs. He explained the general rule of assembling a rub: never use fresh ingredients. Fresh ingredients will cause a rub to clump and limit its shelf life. Always make a batch that will last ten applications—you'll use it on more than just your barbecue. For Archie and Sarge, their rub was the pride of their barbecue. It was a secret recipe passed down and modified to perfection.

Sarge swaggered with arrogance and asked us to guess the ingredients in his dry rub. He didn't think us "Yankees"—as he called us—could ever guess what was in his pride-and-joy dry rub. Being the food geeks that we are, we scraped some into our hands, took a hearty smell, and listed off every single ingredient in his rub while Park wrote it all down in his little notebook. As Sarge realized his mistake, his face crumbled and it looked like he was going to throw up.

The next morning we returned to see how the boys did at the event. They were disappointed with their fourth place finish in the Whole Hog category, but they came in third for Best Ribs. It wasn't a total loss, as there was nothing left to do for everyone but to drink and eat that barbecued hog. It was divine. The meat was succulent, the skin mahogany and crispy. Everything had the flavor of apple wood smoke—all that spritzing paid off. I was told to eat the cheek and, my God, it was like having truffles for the first time. This was a life-altering experience. The flavors from the rub, the apple wood smoke, and the hard work in keeping the temperature constant day and night came together in a piece of delicious, silky pork. Yup, pork is the food of the gods!

The Southern Gentlemen's Culinary Society may have looked intimidating, but they were some of the nicest people we've met down there. We learned so much from those guys. And the following year, they won the Grand Championship of the whole competition.

The Memphis trip was an invaluable lesson in the culture of barbecue. The best part was meeting and talking to people who truly love and nurture barbecue. It is a part of their lives and their community. I will never forget the pit masters' passion for their craft, nor how willing they were to share their knowledge. It was two weeks of immersing ourselves in the details of barbecue with the masters of the South.

We returned to Canada with a notebook full of lists, ingredients, restaurant reviews, and notes and impressions on barbecue culture. We found out which barbecue pit company would work for us in Vancouver and made lots of contacts in the industry.

One week after we returned to Vancouver, we were asked to judge the Pacific Northwest BBQ Association Competition in Woodinville, Washington. We took a crash course on barbecue judging upon arrival at the competition and subsequently judged brisket and ribs. We took our friend David Denyer with us, who photographed us in our glory—you'll see his wonderful photos hanging on the walls of our restaurants.

That same summer we found out that a little diner (one that Vancouverites will remember as a landmark) was selling its business. The former location of the Aristocratic at West Broadway and Granville would become our new home as of September 2001. With the help of our families and friends we created a space of our own—a rustic, funky, crowded little haven.

As it turned out, people were looking for comfort food—we definitely hit a niche. We presented inexpensive and casual dining in a way that Vancouver hadn't seen before. By late September we were already very busy. We got slammed through autumn and winter. And in the spring of the following year, we won the Vancouver Magazine Best New Casual Award. We were ecstatic. And business got even crazier.

What's
Our
Secret?

What's Our Secret?

Traditional barbecue is possibly the most important contribution to Southern cuisine; roadside barbecue joints dot the landscape in almost every Southern state. But what is barbecue?

Barbecue's roots go back to Africa, Mexico, and the Americas. It consists of inexpensive cuts of meat (usually pork) cooked over long periods of time. And it always involves some form of aromatic hardwood smoke.

The concept of cooking meat over coals dates back to prehistoric times. People from almost every continent and culture use hot coals to cook meat. The word itself is likely from the West Indian term *barbacoa*, which indicates a method of slow cooking meats over hot coals. Another origin could very well be derived from the French phrase *barbe à queue*, which can be loosely translated into "from beard to tail" (a whole, roasted animal on a spit). Another claim is that the word came from roadhouse signs that read, "Bar, Beer and Cues."

Okay, so the concept isn't new, but there's definitely something unique about the way those Southerners cook that 'cue. We can't even decide on how to spell the word. Is it *barbecue*? *Barbeque*? However it's spelled, we at Memphis Blues love it and strive to make it the most authentic we can.

Ten things that make it traditional Southern barbecue:

→ The meat isn't preboiled, but cooked over low temperatures for a long time.
→ Dry rubs are generally applied to the meat prior to cooking.
→ Natural lump charcoal (or briquettes) is used as a heat source.
→ The meat is cooked with indirect heat.
→ Natural hardwood smoke is a flavoring agent.
→ Sauce, if used, is applied at the latter stages of cooking or used only as a dipping condiment.
→ Forks, knives, and spoons are optional.
→ The portions are large.

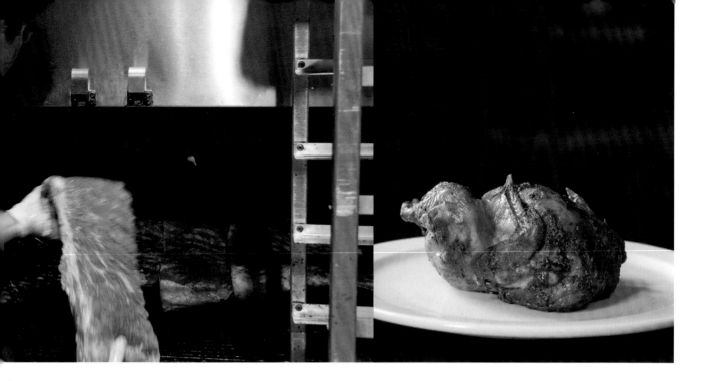

→ Eating in large groups is desirable.

→ Inexpensive, casual, and unpretentious is the order of the day.

We're not going to debate what kind of barbecue is better out of the many styles—we want to focus on Southern barbecue, done slow and low. Barbecue is not just a cuisine, it's a culture!

TYPES OF BARBECUE

Even though there are as many types of authentic barbecue as there are people to make it, there are regional differences.

The East

The Carolinas, Georgia, and Florida are pork shoulder and whole hog country. The regional specialty is pulled pork—and you won't find beef on the menu. The pork shoulder is slow cooked over hickory or seasoned pecan wood, and the dry rubs tend to be sweet and mild.

Sauces vary from spicy vinaigrettes to sweet mustards. Tomato-based sauces are scarce until you get further west. In the Carolinas, when they barbecue a whole hog, it's pretty standard to dress the cooked pork with apple cider vinegar, sugar, and a whole mess of different herbs and seasonings like black pepper, chili flakes, garlic powder, mustard powder, and onion powder. Then everyone gathers around the table and digs in for what they call a "hog pickin'." Mmm!

The Mid-South

Missouri and Tennessee are where the classic St. Louis–style ribs come into their own. The pulled pork is tender and succulent, and the sauces tend to be tomato based, laced with molasses and mustard. The St. Louis–style ribs are long and meaty, with the flesh just coming off the bone. The ribs are often dry-rubbed and cooked for two to three hours over hardwood charcoal. Then they are either served naked (without an accompanying sauce), or glazed at the last minute with a sweet and sour tomato-based sauce.

While in Memphis, we were frequently asked if we wanted our ribs dry or wet. The barbecue purists are adamant that the meat should be naked, so nothing detracts from its flavor. There is also one Mid-South barbecue specialty from Kentucky: barbecued mutton.

The West

Oklahoma, Arkansas, Kansas, and Texas are beef country. But Kansas is also famous for ribs and pulled pork. In Texas, brisket is king, and beef ribs abound. Pork ribs and spicy hot pork sausages are also popular. The wood choice for smoking is usually oak, mesquite, or pecan. And the rubs have a Southwest influence of cumin and hot chilies.

Barbecue dipping sauces tend to be spicy and thinned with vinegar. The beef brisket in Texas is spicy, tender, and juicy inside—slow smoked over charcoal for up to 15 hours. It's easy to dry out over this period of time, but the skilled pit boss should be able to render it tender and succulent. The classic Texas home-style platter is sliced brisket, ribs, and hot links served with a stack of Wonder Bread . . . yum!

MEAT LINGO

At Memphis Blues we use both fresh and frozen meats for our main cuts. Remember, folks: the origins of barbecue are based on low cost and convenience. This isn't highbrow cuisine, it's common-folk food. The ingredients used in the pantry are not fresh or expensive. To give the cuts of meat their succulent flavor, they need long, slow cooking, which tenderizes the meat and renders the fat.

Boston butt or picnic shoulder (a or b)
Perfect for pulled pork. This is the front shoulder of the pig. Get a whole shoulder and ask for it untrimmed. If the whole thing is too big, ask your butcher to cut it in half for you. Freeze the other half. Don't let him trim it! The fat will render out during the many hours of cooking time. Fat is one of the tastiest parts of all cuts of meat. Any butcher will tell you that a well-marbled cut has more flavor and will cook up less dry than a lean one. Don't shy away from fat!

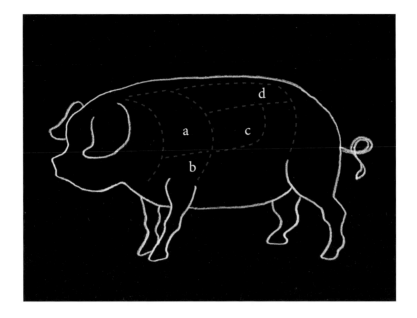

Side ribs (c)

Another name for these is spare ribs. They are trimmed 5 inches (12 cm) in length and have 12 bones; this is referred to as a "St. Louis cut." These are the longest and meatiest of the rib cuts. They come from just above the pig's belly, and if they are custom cut, they should yield two big portions per side. We went through nine or ten suppliers when we first opened the restaurant. It took us a while to be happy with the side profile (thickness) of outside ribs. We were led to understand that most of the meat was trimmed off to make bacon slabs, leaving virtually no meat on the top of the rib! We finally found a supplier who gave us what we wanted. We have stuck with him ever since. Get to know your butcher, establish a relationship with him, and let him know what you need. Getting the right cuts is essential for successful home barbecue.

Baby back ribs (d)

These come from the loin and can be less meaty and more expensive than spare ribs. They are best for grilling because they cook faster. They are toothsome and tender—the flesh melts off the bone. Make sure the side profile is nice and thick. For home barbecue, we often go to the large Chinese chain stores that have a butcher. These guys go through a lot of pork! They will usually give you what you want and the prices are very competitive.

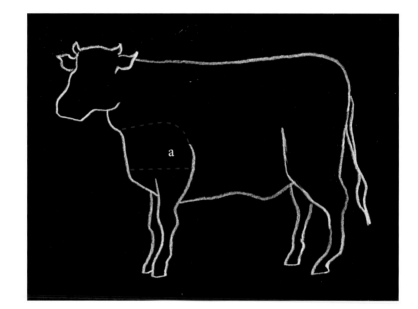

Beef brisket (a)

This is the chest plate on a cow and is difficult to cook successfully. When we first started looking for beef cuts we had a hard time explaining to our suppliers that we wanted fatty cuts of beef. As Vancouver, BC, is a particularly health-conscious city, the only cuts we could get were called "West Coast briskets," a well-trimmed and virtually fat-free piece of meat. Without the fat, the meat tends to dry out during the cooking process. Once we explained to our suppliers that the beef fat would render out during the extremely long cooking process, they finally understood that we really did want untrimmed briskets. We now use exclusively certified Angus briskets that are well known for their marbling and nice thick cap.

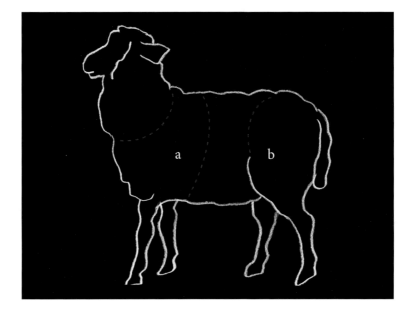

Lamb shoulder (a)

We use lamb from Down Under, but for home barbecuing we recommend that you use local spring lamb. Ask your butcher to remove the bone. The shoulder will then spread out—this is good. Don't tie it up into a roast shape—leave it flat and it will cook up nicely.

Lamb leg (b)

The same goes for this cut as with the lamb shoulder: use local spring lamb. If you'd like a less expensive option, frozen lamb is a good substitute. The stronger the lamb tastes, the better—authentic Kentucky-style lamb is actually mutton.

Chicken

We use small 2–3 lb (1–1.5 kg) line-run fry-ers. These are very young and tender and don't need much cooking time. As with lamb, local, free-range, and/or organic birds are best. A larger bird will be slightly less tender than the little guys, but the beauty of bar-becue is that the longer and slower cooking renders even the toughest cuts soft.

HOME BARBECUE RIGS

Smoking meat is becoming more popular, and there are an increasing number of types of equipment available so that you can smoke your own meat. In our homes, we both have a Weber water smoker, a Weber gas grill, and a basic charcoal barbecue. George has even built a wood-fired oven in his backyard to create the succulent smoky taste in pork.

Please note that most of our barbecue recipes simply cannot be reproduced in the home oven. The smoke is what gives South-ern 'cue its special character and flavor. We provide instructions for making our recipes with both a gas barbecue and a water smok-er. If you're like most folks and you have a gas barbecue, you'll be able to make all of the recipes in this book. Just follow our instruc-tions on how to convert it into a Southern-style smoker.

Gas barbecue

When you use a gas barbecue to smoke, it's all about indirect heat and maintaining a constant temperature. When setting up a home gas barbecue for smoking, you must have a barbecue that has gas jets on both the

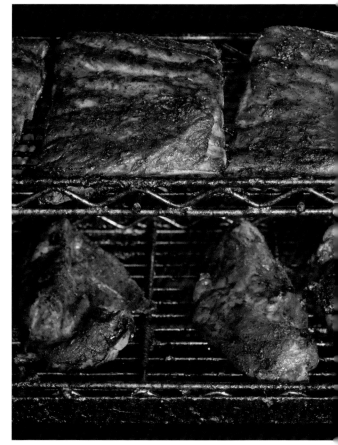

left and right sides, with separate controls. (Most home gas grills are set up like this.)

Turn only one side on to high. Allow it to heat up for a few minutes. When the interior temperature reaches around 300°F (150°C), place a loaded wood chip smoker box (see Tools for Barbecuing on page 43) onto the lit side of the grill (underneath the grill rack, and directly on top of the gas jet cover). This will allow the heat source to ignite the chips and allow them to smolder. To smoke our meat, we've tried using both fruitwood chunks and chips—we prefer chunks. See Wood and Smoking (page 42).

The meat goes on the unlit side of the grill. You will need to reload the smoker box with water-soaked wood chips two or three times during the cooking process. Use a set of tongs and some heavy kitchen mitts to help you remove and replace the smoker box under the grill.

Water smoker
This tool is a bullet-shaped barbecue—tall and skinny like a fat chimney. It has two inset, round pans, one above the other. Above these two pans are two meat racks or stainless steel grates. Above these is a dome-shaped lid. It can be tough to maintain a constant temperature using a water smoker.

Start with lit charcoal in the bottom pan. We suggest using either wood chips or wood chunks on top of the charcoal. This process can be a lot of work, as you need to keep adding HOT charcoal and extra wood as they deplete. The pan above is reserved for liquids. Water is the most commonly used liquid, but any combination of water, beer, wine, fruit juice, or bourbon is acceptable. The liquids help keep the interior of the barbecue moist, which keeps the meat from drying out. The meat is then piled onto the two racks to

smoke. Electric water smokers are also available—ideal for lessening the fuss and work. You still use wood chips, and an electric element slowly cooks the meat. Just add more wood chips if you want a smokier flavor.

Barrel smoker

From the size of this rig, you would think that you could probably cook enough for a small army. This is essentially a 45-gallon drum sawn in half lengthwise. You can use it to grill or smoke. Start with a good bed of hot charcoal and then move it to one end of the barrel. Add logs or wood chunks directly on top of the charcoal. Place your meat onto the grill on the opposite end from the direct heat.

Note that it needs a lot of attention; keeping the heat constant and having to reload the charcoal and wood means you can't stray too far. Most of these rigs are cheaply made and only last three or four years. Some competing barbecue teams swear by the barrel smoker.

Homemade smoker

You can use a discarded and gutted refrigerator (get rid of any plastic, but keep the metal racks) or a clean metal trashcan (slightly tapered) to smoke your meat. Put an electric hotplate on the bottom of your vessel and drill a hole through one side. Run the wire from the hotplate through the hole and into an outlet.

Stack wood chips in a metal pan and place

this on the hotplate. If you're using a trashcan smoker, get yourself a few round metal racks from a barbecue supply store. Measure your trashcan's diameter and get two racks just slightly narrower than the diameter of the lid opening. Slide the racks down inside the opening and tap them into place—the farther down you push them, the tighter they ought to fit. Place the meat onto the metal racks. Shut the door or close the lid, plug in the hotplate, and you're good to go.

Backyard barbecue pit (a mini barrel smoker)

We've seen them sell for $99 at a local hardware store to over $1,500 online. The $99 version will only last a couple of seasons before it becomes a pile of rust in your backyard. The $1,500 version, likely made of stainless steel, will last generations.

In all backyard models, the thermometer is on top and the firebox is separate from the smoke chamber. The pit is generally big enough to hold a large pork shoulder, two to three chickens, or 2 lb (1 kg) of sausages. All the drippings filter to the bottom where a drain plug makes it easy to clean. Under the firebox is a drain for removing ashes. The damper on top of the chimney controls the amount of smoke, allowing you to fine-tune your cooking. A midrange barbecue pit will cost about $600 to $700 and will be made from heavy gauge steel. You can even grill with it.

easy to use, and a far safer alternative to squirting lighter fluid over your coals, which introduces a petroleum flavor to your food. Who wants that?

WOOD AND SMOKING

A variety of wood can be used in making Southern barbecue. The most common types are hickory, oak, pecan, and mesquite. Fruitwood is also used, but you'll find most people use what they have on hand. At Memphis Blues, we use cherry, apple, and walnut (apple's our favorite).

The availability of different woods varies from city to city—the reason we have a great deal of regional variation in barbecue styles. Most barbecue supply stores, large hardware stores, or home renovation stores stock both mesquite and hickory wood chips in small plastic bags specifically for smoking.

If you're going to find your own supply of chips or chunks (or even logs) for home smoking, make sure the wood is chemical free and in pristine form. There should be no mold or fungus of any kind as these can produce off flavors and can be harmful to your health. The wood should have been seasoned for at least one year.

Smoking times are a matter of taste. We

Chimney-style barbecue starter

If you are using lump charcoal, or even briquettes, you should start them with a chimney starter, available at stores that sell barbecues and at some hardware stores. Essentially, this is a small metal chimney with a heatproof handle, a grate about two-thirds of the way to the bottom, and vent holes all over the body. Fill the upper two-thirds with charcoal, roll up three pieces of newspaper and stuff them into the bottom one-third, and touch a match to the newspaper. Place the lit chimney onto your grill, and 20 minutes later you have fully lit coals! These starter chimneys are chemical free,

SHOULD I SOAK?

By not soaking your wood chips in water, you will produce a faster burning and more intense smoke that adds more color to your meat. However, soaking the chips for half an hour causes a slower smoke, and you won't have to reload as often.

recommend using a conservative amount of smoke. When we traveled to Washington State in 2001, we tried quite a few rib joints that had oversmoked their food and used green wood. This produced a flavor of creosote in the meat, which was unpleasant to our palates. To avoid this, make sure you use nicely seasoned wood and use it in moderation. The general rule is one hour of smoking time for every four hours of cooking. Remember to use wood for smoking and not for the heat source.

TOOLS FOR BARBECUING

Aluminum foil (large roll, heavy gauge). A must-have for any backyard barbecue chef. It helps keep meat warm and moist.

Butcher's twine. Use for tying some cuts of meat together during cooking.

Cast-iron Dutch oven (2 quart/2 L). Perfect for braising, or for cooking beans in a gas grill smoker.

Chimney-style barbecue starter. A safer way of starting charcoal than lighter fluid. Easy to use and available at hardware stores.

Drip pans. Eliminates flare-ups and can be used as a water pan to keep meat moist during long smoking times.

Gloves. Great for handling barbecue; stick with the heat-resistant neoprene gloves. Oven mitts get dirty and greasy pretty quickly.

Kitchen tongs (various sizes). Essential for barbecuing. The spring-loaded heavy duty ones are the best and you can buy them at any restaurant supply store. Get two pairs, one for turning cuts of meat and one for moving around wood or charcoal. Using a fork can lead to dryer meat as the juices run out every time you poke it.

Leather gardening gloves. For handling charcoal and wood, and for moving barbecue rigs.

Lump charcoal. Always buy lump charcoal because cheap charcoal may contain petroleum by-products or paraffin, which will add an unpleasant flavor to your barbecue.

Smoker box (available at hardware stores). Inexpensive and great for smoking with your gas grill.

Wood chips (available in bags at hardware stores). Fruit-tree wood is great, but you can also use hickory, pecan, or mesquite. Play around with flavors and stick with your favorite.

	Mon	Tues	Wed	Thur	Fri	Sat	Sun
							4 X
		3		3			2
			3				1
	X	3				3	MIX
	X	X		2			1
			X				1/4
				1		1/2	1

---

⑤ SALAD DRESSING

⑥ BREAD CATFISH

⑦ 1 BATCH OF SPAGHETTI

⑧ RUB DAY/NIGHT LOADS

⑨ MAKE MY RESTAURANT LOOK PRETTY... ✓

---

6 L PS

4 L BBQ SAUCE

GREEN SALAD

1/2 tray of CB - 50 pieces

6 L BEANS.

SATURDAY 22 delivered by 430

- Whitney will deliver pickup

Butt Rub		1/2	1/2	1/2	1/4	1/4	
Brisket Rub	1/2	1/2	1/2	1/2	1/4	1/2 X	
Spicy BBQ Sc.	1	1/2	1/2			1/2 X	
Stock	1		1	1 FULL	1/2	1/2 X	
Soup	2 SB		4 SB	4 B	4 SB	2 X	
Chili	2 SB	2 SB	1 SB		4 SB	4 X	
Collards	5 SB	3 SB	3 SB	3 SB		N/A X	
Bread Seafood	2 TRAY	2 TRAY		1 TRAY	1 TRAY	CAT	
Croutons	1	1		1	1	1/2 X	
				1/2	1/2	1 X	

PANTRY

There's nothing fancy about a barbecue pantry. Usually only dry ingredients are used for rubs and seasonings. Fresh ingredients like herbs, onion, or garlic will clump and limit the shelf life of the rub.

Rubs are generally made in large quantities because in barbecue culture, they are used frequently. You literally put a dry rub on everything. Here's what you'll find in a well-stocked barbecue pantry.

SPICE RACK

garlic powder	smoked salt	ground nutmeg
onion powder	celery salt	cayenne pepper
sweet Spanish paprika	celery seeds	chili flakes
smoked paprika	whole cumin seeds and	chili powder (New
whole peppercorns	ground cumin	Mexico or Ancho)
black pepper, freshly	whole coriander seeds	garam masala
ground and	yellow mustard seeds	five-spice powder
hand sifted	mustard powder (mild	dried oregano
ground white pepper	and hot)	dried parsley
lemon pepper	ground dried ginger	dried rosemary
table salt	ground turmeric	dried sage
sea salt or kosher salt	ground cinnamon	dried cilantro flakes
seasoned salt (we use	ground cloves	dried tarragon
Lawry's)	ground cardamom	bay leaves

CANNED OR BOTTLED GOODS

pork and beans	prepared horseradish
kidney beans	hot sauce (we like Tabasco,
pinto beans	Frank's RedHot, and
black-eyed peas	any Louisiana-style
molasses	hot sauce)
tomato paste	apple cider vinegar
ketchup	red wine vinegar
yellow mustard	white wine vinegar
Dijon mustard	plain white vinegar
soy sauce	liquid honey
Worcestershire sauce	

DRY GOODS

all-purpose flour
yellow cornmeal
granulated sugar
dark brown sugar
demerara sugar

BARBECUE AND WINE

The obvious reply to "What should I drink with barbecue?" Beer. Because of the great American backyard tradition of barbecue, a good ol' brew seems to be pretty well entrenched in the weekend list of preferred beverages. Well, yes, we do sell a lot of beer at Memphis Blues Barbeque. But, we sell a lot of wine, too.

When we first opened, we knew we were going to have a pretty comprehensive wine program. Because of our involvement in the wine business (and overall love of wine), we decided from the get-go to offer a varied selection of affordable but eclectic wine choices. Over the years we have come to realize that when we tell people about wine with barbecue, they grow to love the combination too. As Park teaches in his wine staff seminars, beer quenches your thirst and fills you up with carbohydrates. Wine, on the other hand doesn't fill you up, improves the taste of food, stimulates the appetite, and aids with digestion. In an ideal world, the food flavors are lifted by the wine, and the wine flavors are lifted by the food. What a concept!

The first thing to say about matching wine and barbecue is that we throw all convention out the window. Our favorite pairing with any of our pork dishes is an off-dry German Riesling. We know, this may sound a little strange. Convention may lead you to choose a heavy spicy red with all those bold flavors. Wrong! The greatest complement to pork is apples. The tartness and sweetness of the apple with the rich and salty character of the pork is a match made in heaven. And we've found that German Riesling echoes the apple character almost to a tee.

We love the Selbach Bernkasteler Kurfurstlay 2006 from the Mosel Valley in Germany. This wine has a sweet-sour tartness (or a yin-yang, as our good friend and wine producer Johannes Selbach of Selbach wines in Germany says). Try a good bottle of Riesling with your ribs or pulled pork—you won't be disappointed.

Having said that, not all barbecue goes with Riesling, which is why we have over 15 other wines by the glass in our restaurants. Our favorite reds tend to be Pinot Noir varietals. Although a good Pinot Noir is a lighter-bodied red, it has an intensity of flavor that will stand up to even the boldest of food. It's a versatile and complex wine. The only issue we have with Pinot Noir is that it tends to be hard to find at the right price point (due to its popularity as a result of the movie *Sideways*). When you find one that works for you, buy lots! One of the Pinot Noirs we carry is from Mount Boucherie Estate Winery from Westbank, British Columbia.

Generally, we try to follow one of two principles when matching food with wine:

1. *Opposites attract.* Choose a wine that contrasts with the flavors in the food. For example, a piece of deep-fried fish (which is heavy and rich) goes well with a high-acid wine such as a lemony Sauvignon Blanc.

2. *But similarities sometimes work, too.* Try choosing a wine that echoes the flavor in the food. For example, a big, bold, beefy wine (like an Australian Shiraz) goes well with brisket and lamb. The slightly gamey and strong flavors of the meat are echoed in the big, spicy, and brambly flavors of the wine.

So, when putting together a party selection, mix it up a bit. Try some of the concepts mentioned above, and try a few offbeat selections. You can organize a party around the concept. Experiment, but above all, try barbecue with wine. Your palate will thank you.

Dry Rubs and Wet Mops

DRY RUBS

A dry rub is a mixture of herbs and spices rubbed on a cut of meat before it's barbecued. Some people rub the night before and refrigerate, while others rub just before they put the meat in the pit. The choice is yours.

There are two purposes of the rub: one is to season the meat, and two is to form a protective crust on the surface of the meat to avoid moisture loss while cooking. The dark brown crust that forms, called the "bark," actually keeps the meat juicier on the inside.

Here we've given you a few classic rubs that we use at Memphis Blues. Keep in mind, there are many types of rubs. Be creative and make up your own once you've mastered the technique. The general principle is a balance of salt, sweet, and savory.

All-Purpose Dry Rub

This is the classic, master dry rub that we use at the restaurant. You'll see it in the beans, pork, catfish breading, shrimp, and on our french fries. Try it on homemade snacks, like spiced nuts or popcorn, or on a variety of salads and dressings. Use your imagination! For an average family barbecue, you'll only need 1–2 cups (250–500 mL). However, because this keeps well, and you can use the leftovers in a lot of other recipes, we have included a recipe that makes extra.

MAKES 4 CUPS (1 L)

1 cup (250 mL) dried parsley
1 cup (250 mL) sugar
1 cup (250 mL) Lawry's Seasoned Salt
3 Tbsp (45 mL) ground black pepper
3 Tbsp (45 mL) garlic powder
3 Tbsp (45 mL) onion powder
3 Tbsp (45 mL) dried oregano
3 Tbsp (45 mL) sweet paprika
1 Tbsp (15 mL) mild mustard powder
1 Tbsp (15 mL) celery salt
a pinch of cayenne pepper

Combine all the ingredients in a mixing bowl with a whisk. Make sure there are no clumps. Store any leftover rub in an airtight container in the cupboard for up to 6 months. **USE ON PORK, CHICKEN, TURKEY, OR FISH.**

Tot's Moroccan Barbecue Spice Rub

This is a recipe from Park's brother, Totton. It's a classic rub that evokes the flavors of North Africa. It's very aromatic and versatile.

MAKES 2 CUPS (500 ML)

1 Tbsp + 1 tsp (20 mL) whole cumin seeds
1 Tbsp (15 mL) whole coriander seeds
1 Tbsp (15 mL) whole peppercorns
1 Tbsp (15 mL) cayenne pepper
2 tsp (10 mL) ground turmeric
2 tsp (10 mL) ground cinnamon
2 tsp (10 mL) ground cardamom
1 tsp (5 mL) ground cloves
½ tsp (2 mL) ground ginger
½ tsp (2 mL) sea salt
a pinch of ground nutmeg

In a dry skillet, roast the cumin seeds, coriander seeds, and whole peppercorns over medium heat for 2 minutes. Combine this and the rest of the ingredients in an electric spice grinder. Blend until it becomes a fine powder. Store any leftover rub in an airtight container in the cupboard for up to 6 months.
USE ON PORK, CHICKEN, OR LAMB.

Indian Barbecue Rub

We have many Indian staff members who have been with us a long time. They often bring us food from the temple or from home to share. This rub is inspired by those exotic flavors. MAKES 2 CUPS (500 ML)

¼ cup (60 mL) ground turmeric
¼ cup (60 mL) brown sugar
¼ cup (60 mL) sweet paprika powder
3 Tbsp (45 mL) Lawry's Seasoned Salt
2 Tbsp (30 mL) ground black pepper
2 Tbsp (30 mL) ground coriander
2 Tbsp (30 mL) garam masala
2 Tbsp (30 mL) ground dried ginger
1 Tbsp (15 mL) garlic powder
1 Tbsp (15 mL) cayenne pepper
1 Tbsp (15 mL) ground cumin
1 Tbsp (15 mL) chili flakes
1 Tbsp (15 mL) celery salt

Combine all the ingredients in a large bowl. Mix well to ensure there are no lumps. Store any leftover rub in an airtight container in the cupboard for up to 6 months. USE ON BEEF, PORK, OR LAMB.

Five-Spice Chinese Rub

Since George is Chinese and the two of us came together over food, this recipe is a tribute to the Chinese aspect of our business.
MAKES 2 CUPS (500 ML)

¼ cup (60 mL) sweet paprika powder
3 Tbsp (45 mL) five-spice powder
3 Tbsp (45 mL) sugar
3 Tbsp (45 mL) sea salt
2 Tbsp (30 mL) dried cilantro flakes
2 Tbsp (30 mL) ground dried ginger
1 Tbsp (15 mL) ground white pepper
1 Tbsp (15 mL) garlic powder
1 Tbsp (15 mL) onion powder
1 Tbsp (15 mL) celery salt
1 Tbsp (15 mL) mustard powder

Combine all the ingredients in a large bowl. Mix well to ensure there are no lumps. This rub can be stored in an airtight container in the cupboard for up to 6 months. USE ON BEEF, PORK, CHICKEN, OR SEAFOOD.

Seafood Rub

This rub is a little more delicate, with a perfume-like aroma and a gentle hint of licorice and lemon. **MAKES 2 CUPS (500 ML)**

¼ cup (60 mL) smoked salt
2 Tbsp (30 mL) granulated sugar
2 Tbsp (30 mL) garlic powder
2 Tbsp (30 mL) lemon pepper
1 Tbsp (15 mL) onion powder
1 Tbsp (15 mL) celery salt
1 Tbsp (15 mL) dried tarragon
1 Tbsp (15 mL) dried parsley

Combine all the ingredients in a large bowl. Mix well to ensure there are no lumps. This rub can be stored in an airtight container in the cupboard for up to 6 months. **USE ON SALMON OR OTHER SEAFOOD.**

Brisket Rub

When we developed the recipes from our trip to Memphis in May, we didn't have a set plan for beef. All of our recipes were centered around pork; Memphis is a pork town. When we decided to balance out the menu with a beef item, we decided that a stronger rub would be needed to pair with the bolder taste of beef brisket. This is the rub we came up with, and our brisket is still a favorite in all of our restaurants.

MAKES 2 CUPS (500 ML)

¼ cup (60 mL) sweet paprika
¼ cup (60 mL) Lawry's Seasoned Salt
¼ cup (60 mL) dried parsley
1 Tbsp (15 mL) dark brown sugar
1 Tbsp (15 mL) garlic powder
1 Tbsp (15 mL) onion powder
1 Tbsp (15 mL) dried oregano
1 Tbsp (15 mL) ground black pepper
1 tsp (5 mL) mustard powder
1 tsp (5 mL) cayenne pepper
1 tsp (5 mL) celery salt
a large pinch of ground cumin
a large pinch of chili flakes

Combine all the ingredients in a large bowl. Mix well to ensure there are no lumps. Store in an airtight container in the cupboard for up to 6 months. USE ON BEEF, GAME, OR LAMB.

WET MOPS

We don't mop in our restaurant, but wet mops are an important part of home barbecuing. The reason we don't mop is that our commercial barbecue pit treats the food differently than a home pit. We cook so much meat at a time that the interior of the pit is quite humid, and therefore our cuts don't need extra moisture. At home, it is more challenging to keep your cuts from drying out. That's what mops are for.

Mops also enhance flavor. They are generally a combination of liquids and spices that are brushed onto the meat during the barbecuing process. They are different from a sauce, in that they are thinner and not sweet in nature. You can use a basting tube or a barbecue brush to apply a mop. Specialty barbecue stores sell a miniature mop device especially for this purpose. Beware of adding anything too sweet to your mop as it will caramelize and burn during the cooking process.

Basic Wet Mop

This is a simple, all-purpose wet mop that will allow you to maintain moisture in your meat during the smoking process.

MAKES 2 CUPS (500 ML)

1 cup (250 mL) lager beer
1 cup (250 mL) apple juice
¼ cup (60 mL) molasses
2 Tbsp (30 mL) brown sugar

Combine all the ingredients in a heavy saucepan over medium heat. Stir until the molasses and sugar dissolve. This should be used the day you make it.

VARIATIONS
→ To the above mixture add 1 ounce (30 mL) of bourbon whiskey.
→ To the above mixture add 1 cup (250 mL) yellow mustard.
→ To the above mixture add ¼ cup (60 mL) Tabasco sauce.
→ Substitute dark ale, stout, or hard apple cider for the lager.

Horseradish Beef Brisket Mop

Ever had beef with horseradish? Try cooking it with horseradish. It's yummy. MAKES 2½ CUPS (625 ML)

1 cup (250 mL) red wine
1 cup (250 mL) redcurrant jelly
½ cup (125 mL) prepared horseradish

In a heavy saucepan, whisk together all the ingredients. Place the saucepan over medium heat, whisking constantly, for 4 minutes or until the jelly is melted. This should be used up the day you make it.

VARIATIONS
→ Use port wine instead of dry red wine.
→ To the above mixture add a couple of pinches of dried herbs like oregano or rosemary.
→ To the above mixture add a pinch or two of garlic powder.

Lamb Mop

Lamb with mint, rosemary, and black pepper . . . classic flavors.

MAKES 1½ CUPS (375 ML)

1 cup (250 mL) red wine
¼ cup (60 mL) chopped fresh mint
¼ cup (60 mL) chopped fresh or dried rosemary
2 cloves fresh garlic, minced
2 Tbsp (30 mL) ground black pepper

Mix all the ingredients in a bowl until well combined. This will keep in the refrigerator for up to 2 days.

Dry Rubs and Wet Mops

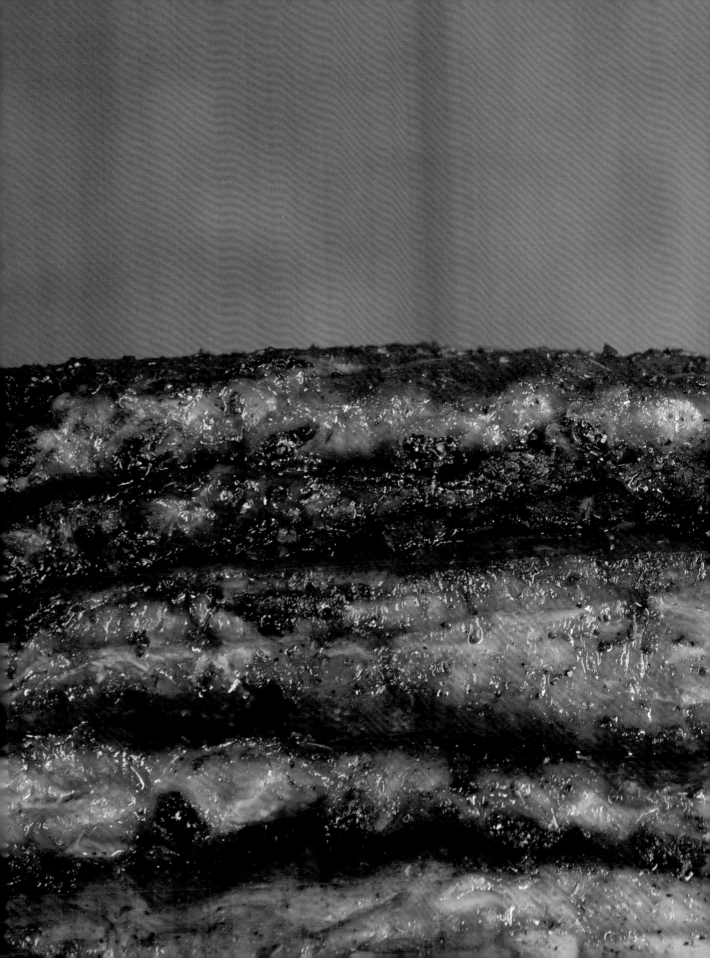

Meat

Meat

Pulled Pork

Follow this recipe and you will be in barbecue heaven! This is our signature dish, our staple. If you don't have a barbecue or smoker, see page 70 for our Oven-Roasted Pulled Pork recipe. **MAKES 8 SERVINGS**

5 lb (2.2 kg) pork shoulder or picnic shoulder
½ cup (125 mL) All-Purpose Dry Rub (page 54)
six 3- x 3-inch (8 x 8 cm) chunks apple wood
       OR
one 2 lb (1 kg) bag of wood chips if smoking with a smoker box

GAS BARBECUE METHOD

Rub the pork shoulder with the dry rub. Make sure the shoulder is well coated on all sides. Turn on one side of the gas barbecue to create a temperature of 250–275°F (120–140°C). Put one piece of apple wood on the lit side of the grill. (Or, use a smoker box and refill as needed.)

Place the shoulder on the unlit side of the grill, fat side up. Close the lid and allow it to smoke. Once the smoke has cleared, open the lid and put in another chunk of wood. Repeat this smoking technique until all the wood is gone. A 5 lb (2.2 kg) pork shoulder will take approximately 8 hours to become soft enough to pull apart. During the last hour of cooking, tightly wrap the meat in tinfoil to allow the shoulder to steam in its own moisture.

Take the meat off the barbecue and let it stand for 20 minutes. Remove the tinfoil and place the meat in a large stainless steel bowl. Use your hands to break the meat up into tiny pieces (a kneading motion similar to making bread works well). Incorporate all the fat and juices into the meat mixture. Use right away or package it in plastic wrap (to retain moisture) for later use. Keeps refrigerated for up to 2 weeks, or frozen for several months.

WATER SMOKER METHOD

Start the charcoal in a starter chimney. Make sure the coals are white and hot before loading. Fill the water reservoir half full. Load the charcoal into the smoker and place 2 chunks of wood on it. Or, use handfuls of wood chips placed directly on the charcoal. Place the pork shoulder on the top rack of the smoker, fat side up. Close the lid and allow it to smoke. Keep adding hot charcoal and wood as it burns down. You may need to reload 3 or 4 times during the 8 hours. Monitor the temperature and try to keep it consistently between 250–275°F (120–140°C). During the last hour of cooking, wrap the meat in tinfoil to retain its moisture. Serve as above.

Oven-Roasted Pulled Pork

Pick a pork shoulder that's not too lean, because you will render the fat through the lean meat during the long roasting time. You'll lose up to 30% of the raw weight when it's done. Even in the oven, expect about 4–4½ hours of cooking time. It's slow food—don't rush it!

MAKES 6 SERVINGS

4 lb (2 kg) boneless pork shoulder or picnic shoulder
¼ cup (60 ml) All-Purpose Dry Rub (page 54)

Preheat oven to 225°F (105°C).

Rub the pork shoulder liberally with the All-Purpose Dry Rub. Place the shoulder in a roasting pan, fat cap up, and cook in the preheated oven for 3 hours. Remove from the oven, wrap with tinfoil, and cook for another hour. To know when it's done, test it by pushing down on the pork shoulder. It should feel tender and ready to fall apart. If it's still too firm, cook for another 30 minutes.

Remove from the oven and unwrap the pork. Use two forks to separate the pork while it rests in the roasting pan. There will be natural juices and drippings that you can incorporate back into the pulled pork. Just massage them in with your hands (clean, of course!). This will add extra flavor and keep it nice and moist. Serve on a bun, with a salad, or as a meal. It's versatile!

Pulled Pork Pizza

One of Elvis's favorites! Quick and easy to make. MAKES 1 LARGE PIZZA

one 14-inch (35 cm) pizza shell or frozen pizza dough
5 oz (150 mL) pizza sauce or puréed tomatoes
12 oz (350 g) Pulled Pork (page 68)
½ lb (250 g) shredded mozzarella cheese

Preheat oven to 475°F (240°C). If you're using a pizza stone, preheat it in the oven.

If using frozen pizza dough, let it thaw and roll it out to be approximately 14 inches (35 cm) on a floured counter. Transfer the pizza to a pizza pan if you aren't using a pizza stone. Spread the pizza sauce evenly over the dough, leaving a ¼-inch (5 mm) border. Evenly spread the pulled pork on the pizza and sprinkle the cheese overtop. Slide the pizza in the preheated oven (directly onto the hot pizza stone if using) and bake for 12 minutes, or just until the edges of the crust brown and the cheese bubbles.

VARIATIONS
Add mushrooms, onions, tomatoes, or any other toppings of your choice. You can also substitute beef brisket, smoked chicken, or double smoked farmer's sausage for the pulled pork.

Pulled Pork Quesadillas

These are quick and simple—especially with leftover pulled pork. George's kids love them. MAKES 4 SERVINGS

½ bunch fresh cilantro
4 green onions
8 large flour tortillas
2 cups (500 mL) shredded mozzarella (or any cheese of your choice)
1 lb (500 g) Pulled Pork (page 68)

Chop the cilantro and green onion and mix together in a bowl. Set aside. Lay out 4 tortilla shells and divide the pulled pork evenly between them. Top each one with some of the cheese. Sprinkle on the green onion and cilantro mix and place the remaining 4 tortilla shells on top of the loaded ones. Gently press down on each so the filling doesn't fall out when you move them.

Cook the quesadillas one at a time in a nonstick skillet over medium heat. (Each side takes about 3 minutes.) Once the cheese is melted and it's heated through, remove from the skillet and cut into 4 triangles.

Serve with salsa, hot sauce, and sour cream.

VARIATION
You can substitute Smoked Chicken meat (page 96) for the pulled pork.

Carolina-Style Pulled Pork Sandwich

A great sandwich! The vinegar and chili really give it a kick and cut the richness of the Pulled Pork. MAKES 4 SANDWICHES

1½ lb (750 g) Pulled Pork (page 68)
2 Tbsp (30 mL) Brisket Rub (page 59)
¼ cup (60 mL) apple cider vinegar
1 tsp (5 mL) chili flakes
⅓ cup (75 mL) Creamy Coleslaw (page 157)
4 large white hamburger buns, cut in half

In a medium mixing bowl, combine the Pulled Pork, Brisket Rub, vinegar, and chili flakes. Mix well. Spread 1 heaping Tbsp (15 mL) of the Creamy Coleslaw on the bottom half of each bun. Pile 6 oz (175 g) of Pulled Pork on top of the coleslaw and place the tops back on the buns. Serve with potato chips.

Meat

Memphis Pulled Pork Sandwich

Without this sandwich, we would have no business selling barbecue. In Memphis, when you go into a barbecue joint and ask for a barbecue sandwich, you get pulled pork . . . there isn't any other kind!

MAKES 4 SANDWICHES

1½ lb (750 g) Pulled Pork (page 68)
1 cup (250 mL) Memphis Blues Classic Barbecue Sauce (page 122)
1 cup (250 mL) Creamy Coleslaw (page 157)
4 large white hamburger buns, cut in half

Reheat the Pulled Pork in the oven or in the microwave. In a small saucepan, heat the Memphis Blues Classic Barbecue Sauce. Pile the Creamy Coleslaw on the bottom half of the bun. Divide the warm meat into 4 portions and heap onto the slaw, then smother with as much sauce as you like. Now dig in! Try to have just one . . .

At our restaurant, Park tells our customers to imagine the white burger bun as a blank canvas about to become the masterpiece. It's all about the barbecue, not the bread.

Pork Side Ribs

Another name for these is spare ribs. The St. Louis cut is the longest and meatiest of the rib cuts. These ribs come from just above the pig's belly, and if they are custom cut, they should yield two big portions per side. If you don't have time to make this version, try our Cheater Ribs recipe (page 79). **MAKES 4 SERVINGS**

4 lb (2 kg) rack of St. Louis–cut pork side ribs
1 cup (250 mL) All-Purpose Dry Rub (page 54)
three 3- x 3-inch (8 x 8 cm) chunks apple wood
      OR
one 1 lb (500 g) bag of wood chips if using a smoker box

GAS BARBECUE METHOD

Rub the meat with the All-Purpose Dry Rub. Make sure the ribs are well coated on all sides. Turn on one side of the gas barbecue to create a temperature of 275–300°F (140–150°C). Put one piece of apple wood on the lit side of the grill. (Or, use a smoker box and refill with wood as needed.)

Place the meat on the unlit side of the grill, fat side up. Close the lid and allow it to smoke. Once the smoke has cleared, open the lid and put another chunk of wood in. Repeat this smoking technique until all the wood is gone. A 2 lb (1 kg) rack will take approximately 3 hours to become tender. The way to check doneness is to gently bend the rack in half. If the meat breaks easily and just starts to come away from the bone, it's done. During the last 30 minutes of cooking, tightly wrap the meat in tinfoil to allow it to steam in its own moisture.

Take the meat off the barbecue and allow it to stand for 10 minutes. Remove the tinfoil and flip the rack over on its back so the rib bones are clearly visible. Using these bones as a guide, slice the ribs into individual portions and serve with Memphis Blues Classic Barbecue Sauce (page 122) on the side.

Meat

Pork Side Ribs (CONT'D)

WATER SMOKER METHOD

Start the charcoal in a starter chimney. Make sure the coals are white and hot before loading. Fill the water reservoir half full. Load the charcoal into the smoker and place 2 chunks of wood on it. Or, use handfuls of wood chips placed directly on the charcoal. Put rib rack on the top rack of the smoker, skin side down. Close the lid and allow it to smoke. Keep adding hot charcoal and wood as it burns down. You may need to reload 3 or 4 times during the 8 hours. Monitor the temperature to keep it between 275–300°F (140–150°C). During the last hour of cooking, wrap the meat in tinfoil to retain its moisture. Serve as above.

Cheater Ribs

Don't get us wrong, folks—real barbecue takes a commitment of considerable time and effort. But, most people don't have as much time as it takes to cook authentic barbecue. So for those who need a hit of barbecue, but are low on time, this recipe will knock a few hours off.

MAKES 4 SERVINGS

2 sides of baby back ribs
1 cup (250 mL) Memphis Blues Classic Barbecue Sauce (page 122)
a handful of hickory wood chips

Preheat the oven to 400°F (200°C). With a brush, apply the Memphis Blues Classic Barbecue Sauce to the ribs until evenly coated. Tightly wrap and seal the ribs in heavy tinfoil. Place the meat in the preheated oven and bake for 1½ hours.

Soak the hickory chips in a bowl of hot water for 15 minutes, then place them in a tin pie plate. Turn on one side of the gas barbecue to create a temperature of 300°F (150°C). When the meat is ready to come out of the oven and go on the grill, put the wood chips (in the tin pie plate) directly over the flame (underneath the grill but on top of the gas jet cover). Unwrap the ribs and place them on the unlit side of the smoker. Close the lid and smoke for 15 minutes, or until the smoke has cleared.

Slide the meat over to the lit side of the barbecue and grill the meat for another 10 minutes, being careful not to burn it (you may need to turn the gas down at this point). When the ribs are nicely caramelized and sizzling, serve immediately.

Smoked Pork Shank

We serve the pork shanks as a special on some cold winter nights. They are comforting, tender, and delicious. MAKES 4 SERVINGS

four 1½ lb (750 g) pork shanks
¾ cup (175 mL) Brisket Rub (page 59)
three 3- x 3-inch (8 x 8 cm) chunks apple wood
         OR
one 1 lb (500 g) bag of wood chips if smoking with a smoker box

GAS BARBECUE METHOD

Rub the meat with the Brisket Rub. Make sure the shanks are well coated on all sides; sprinkle some rub into the cavity. Turn on one side of the gas barbecue to create a temperature of 275–300°F (140–150°C). Put one piece of apple wood on the lit side of the grill. (Or use a smoker box and refill as needed.)

Place the meat on the unlit side of the grill. Close the lid and allow it to smoke. Once the smoke has cleared, open the lid and put another chunk of wood in. Repeat this smoking technique until all the wood is gone. The 4 shanks will take approximately 2–2½ hours to smoke. During the last hour of cooking, tightly wrap the meat in tinfoil to allow the shanks to steam in their own moisture. When the meat starts to fall off the bone, it's ready.

Take the meat off the barbecue and let it stand for 10 minutes. Remove the tinfoil and serve on a bed of Southwest-Style Pit Beans (page 136).

WATER SMOKER METHOD

Start the charcoal in a starter chimney. Make sure the coals are white and hot before loading. Fill the water reservoir half full. Load the charcoal into the smoker and place in 2 chunks of wood. Or, use handfuls of wood chips placed directly on the charcoal.

Place the shanks on the top rack of the smoker, close the lid, and allow them to smoke. Keep adding hot charcoal and wood as it burns down. You may need to reload 2 times during the hour. Keep the temperature between 275–300°F (140–150°C). Serve as above.

Black-Eyed Peas and Pork Belly

There is no more authentic Southern soul food than black-eyed peas and pork belly. This is a warming, hearty dish, great for those early winter days before the snow flies. **MAKES 4 SERVINGS**

½ medium onion
1 Tbsp (15 mL) vegetable oil
one 28 oz (796 mL) can black-eyed peas
1 cup (250 mL) Memphis Blues Smoky Chicken Stock (page 168)
6 cloves garlic
1 lb (500 g) pork belly
1 Tbsp (15 mL) Brisket Rub (page 59)

Chop the onion into a medium dice. Add the onion and oil to a cast-iron Dutch oven (or any heavy flameproof casserole dish) and fry over medium heat until tender. Remove from the heat and mix in the black-eyed peas, Memphis Blues Smoky Chicken Stock, and garlic. Rub the pork belly with the Brisket Rub and place on top of the peas.

Turn on one side of the gas barbecue to create a temperature of 250–275°F (120–140°C). Put one piece of apple wood on the lit side of the grill. (Or, use a smoker box and refill as needed.) Remove the Dutch oven from the heat and with the lid off, place on the unlit side of the barbecue. Load the smoker box with wood chips, close the lid, and smoke the casserole for 4 hours or until the pork is tender enough to fall apart. Change the smoker box 3 times for a good smoky flavor.

Beef Brisket

Our brisket has gotten better over the years. It started out good, and now it's fabulous! Why? We switched to certified Angus beef about 4 years ago and it has an awesome marble. Yummm. MAKES 8 SERVINGS

5 lb (2.2 kg) brisket
½ cup (125 mL) Brisket Rub (page 59)
six 3- x 3-inch (8 x 8 cm) chunks apple wood
     OR
one 2 lb (1 kg) bag of wood chips if smoking with a smoker box

Meat

Beef Brisket (CONT'D)

GAS BARBECUE METHOD

Rub the meat with Brisket Rub. Make sure the brisket is well coated on all sides. Turn on one side of the gas barbecue to create a temperature of 250–275°F (120–140°C). Put one piece of apple wood on the lit side of the grill. (Or, use a smoker box and refill as needed.)

Place the meat on the unlit side of the grill, fat side up. Close the lid and allow to it to smoke. Once the smoke has cleared, open the lid and put in another chunk of wood. Repeat this smoking technique until all the wood is gone. A 5 lb (2.2 kg) brisket will take approximately 8 hours to become tender enough to slice easily. During the last hour of cooking, tightly wrap the meat in tinfoil to allow the brisket to steam in its own moisture.

Take the meat off the barbecue and let it stand for 20 minutes. Remove the tinfoil and either use right away or package it in plastic wrap (to retain moisture) for later use. Keeps refrigerated for up to 2 weeks, or frozen for several months.

WATER SMOKER METHOD

Start the charcoal in a starter chimney. Make sure the coals are white and hot before loading. Fill the water reservoir half full. Load the charcoal into the smoker and place 2 chunks of wood on it. Or, use handfuls of wood chips placed directly on the charcoal. Place the brisket on the top rack of the smoker, fat side up. Close the lid and allow it to smoke. Keep adding hot charcoal and wood as it burns down. You may need to reload 3 or 4 times during the 8 hours. Monitor the temperature and try to keep it consistently between 250–275°F (120–140°C). During the last hour of cooking, wrap the meat in tinfoil to retain its moisture. Serve as above.

Smoked Beef Ribs

When we introduced these beauties to our daily specials, we couldn't believe how popular they were. They always sell out, and in the rare case that they don't, the leftovers make a delicious boneless sandwich the next day. A whole beef short rib comes with 3 bones in it—that's why this recipe makes 3 servings. **MAKES 3 SERVINGS**

one 7 lb (3.15 kg) beef short rib plate (3 bones)
¾ cup (175 mL) Brisket Rub (page 59)
five 3- x 3-inch (8 x 8 cm) chunks apple wood
       OR
one 2 lb (1 kg) bag of wood chips if smoking with a smoker box

GAS BARBECUE METHOD

Rub the rib plate with Brisket Rub. Make sure it's well coated on all sides. Turn on one side of the gas barbecue to create a temperature of 300–325°F (150–160°C). Put 2 pieces of wood on the lit side of the grill. (Or, use a smoker box and refill as needed.)

Place the rib plate on the unlit side of the grill, meat side up. Close the lid and allow to it to smoke. Once the smoke has cleared, open the lid and put another chunk of wood in. Repeat this smoking technique until all the wood is gone. A 7 lb (3.15 kg) rib plate will take approximately 4 hours to become tender. During the last hour of cooking, tightly wrap the meat in tinfoil to steam in its own moisture. Remove from the heat and let it stand for 10 minutes. Remove the tinfoil and slice between the bones. The ribs should be so tender they slide off the bone. Serve with Memphis Blues Pit Beans (page 134), Tangy Slaw (page 159), and Warm Potato Salad (page 153).

WATER SMOKER METHOD

Start the charcoal in a starter chimney. Make sure the coals are white and hot before loading. Fill the water reservoir half full. Load the charcoal into the smoker and place 2 chunks of wood on it. Or, use handfuls of wood chips placed directly on the charcoal. Put the plate on the top rack of the smoker, meat side up. Close the lid and allow it to smoke for 4 hours. Keep adding hot charcoal and wood as it burns down. You may need to reload 3 or 4 times during the cooking time. Keep the temperature between 300–325°F (150–160°C). Serve as above.

Meat

Homemade
Sausage Patties

This is a simple homemade sausage meat recipe that you could force into sausage casings, but making homemade sausages is a whole other book, and requires a lot of special equipment. If you want to use this homemade sausage meat recipe on the home smoker, just form the mixture into patties and put them straight onto the unlit side of the gas grill. MAKES 10 SMALL SAUSAGE PATTIES

2 lb (1 kg) boneless pork shoulder, untrimmed and ground
½ cup (125 mL) freshly ground dried fennel seeds
1 Tbsp (15 mL) ground black pepper
1 tsp (5 mL) minced fresh garlic
1 Tbsp (15 mL) sweet paprika
1 Tbsp + 2 tsp (25 mL) kosher salt

Combine all the ingredients in a large mixing bowl until well blended. Chill in the refrigerator for 2 hours. Once chilled, form the mixture into 3 oz (75 g) patties. Place one patty on a small sheet of wax paper, and place another piece of wax paper on top. Alternate patties and wax paper until you have formed all the meat.

These are best used straightaway, but you can refrigerate overnight if necessary. Turn on one side of the gas barbecue to create a temperature of 300°F (150°C). Place the patties on the unlit side of the grill and load the lit side with a smoker box filled with wood chips. Smoke the patties 45 minutes.

Smoked Sausages

If you've got time on your hands, you can make your own link sausages. If you don't, just buy a few pounds of fresh Italian sausages. The sausages we use—Alberta farmer's sausages—are double smoked. We love 'em! MAKES 4 SERVINGS

3 lb (1.5 kg) Italian pork sausages (mild or hot)
two 3- x 3-inch (8 x 8 cm) chunks apple wood
     OR
one 1 lb (500 g) bag of wood chips if smoking with a smoker box

Smoked Sausages (CONT'D)

GAS BARBECUE METHOD

Turn on one side of the gas barbecue to create a temperature of 275–300°F (140–150°C). Put one piece of apple wood on the lit side of the grill. (Or, use a smoker box and refill as needed.)

Place the meat on the unlit side of the grill. Close the lid and allow to it to smoke. Once the smoke has cleared, open the lid and put another chunk in. Repeat this smoking technique until all the wood is gone. Two pounds (1 kg) of sausages will take approximately 1 hour to cook through. To check doneness, gently slice into a sausage. If the meat is no longer pink in the middle, it's done. Slice the sausages and serve with either North Carolina Mustard Sauce (page 126) or Memphis Blues Classic Barbecue Sauce (page 122).

WATER SMOKER METHOD

Start the charcoal in a starter chimney. Make sure the coals are white and hot before loading. Fill the water reservoir half full. Load the charcoal into the smoker and place 2 chunks of wood on it. Or, use handfuls of wood chips placed directly on the charcoal. Put the sausages on the top rack of the smoker, close the lid, and allow them to smoke. Keep adding hot charcoal and wood as it burns down. You may need to reload once during the 1 hour. Keep the temperature between 275–300°F (140–150°C). Serve as above.

Joseph's Singapore Chicken Wings

Joseph is a chef who shared this recipe with us, and we've used it for home barbecue functions on many occasions. These wings are sweet, hot, sour, and salty. MAKES 6 SERVINGS

3 lb (1.5 kg) trimmed chicken wings
2 Tbsp (30 mL) canola oil
3 cloves garlic
one 1-inch (2.5 cm) piece fresh ginger
1 cup (250 mL) tomato paste
1 cup (250 mL) dark brown sugar
½ cup (125 mL) hoisin sauce
½ cup (125 mL) soy sauce
½ cup (125 mL) ketchup
2 Tbsp (30 mL) chili paste

Preheat the barbecue to medium heat. In a stainless steel bowl, toss the chicken with the canola oil. Place the chicken wings onto the preheated barbecue, turning frequently until the wings are cooked through and golden brown.

While the wings are cooking, mince the garlic and ginger. Add the remaining ingredients in a large bowl and whisk to remove any lumps.

Remove the cooked wings from the grill and toss them in the sauce. Make sure they are thoroughly coated, then place them back on the grill. Look out for flare-ups! Once the wings are reheated, serve piping hot.

Meat

Dry-Rubbed Rotisserie Chicken

We often use a dry rub to season a chicken before putting it on the rotisserie. This is another great way to use your up your All-Purpose Dry Rub. SERVES 4

one 3 lb (1.5 kg) roasting chicken
¼ cup (60 mL) All-Purpose Dry Rub (page 54)

Set up the barbecue rotisserie and preheat the gas barbecue to 350°F (180°C).

Rinse the chicken in cold water and pat dry with a paper towel. Sprinkle the entire chicken with the All-Purpose Dry Rub (even in the cavity). Secure the chicken to the rotisserie bar and place onto the barbecue. Make sure you place a drip pan under the chicken to avoid flare-ups. Close the lid and turn on the rotisserie. Cook the chicken for 1 hour. To check for doneness, pull on a leg. If it comes apart easily and the juices run clear, it's ready.

Remove the chicken from the rotisserie and it let stand for 10 minutes before carving.

VARIATION
Add a smoker box to the grill, filled with cherry or apple wood. It will definitely kick up the smoky flavor. And you can add diced potatoes and ¾ cup (175 mL) of chicken stock to the drip pan during the cooking so you can have great potatoes to serve on the side.

Meat

Smoked Chicken

This is truly one of the easiest recipes to make at home. When we do barbecue demonstrations we always include a poultry recipe because it's quick, simple, and is perfect for up to six people on a home barbecue. **MAKES 4 TO 6 SERVINGS**

two 2 lb (1 kg) frying chickens
¾ cup (175 mL) All-Purpose Dry Rub (page 54)
three 3- x 3-inch (8 x 8 cm) chunks apple wood
            OR
one 1 lb (500 g) bag of wood chips if smoking with a smoker box

GAS BARBECUE METHOD

Rub the chickens with the All-Purpose Dry Rub. Make sure the chicken is well coated on all sides. Sprinkle some rub into the cavity. Turn on one side of the gas barbecue to create a temperature of 275–300°F (140–150°C). Put one piece of wood on the lit side of the grill. (Or, use a smoker box and refill as needed.)

Place the meat on the unlit side of the grill, breast side up. Close the lid and allow it to smoke. Once the smoke has cleared, open the lid and put another chunk of wood in. Repeat this smoking technique until all the wood is gone. The chicken will take approximately 2–2½ hours to smoke. To check for doneness, pull on a leg. If it wiggles freely and the juices run clear, it's ready.

Take the chickens off the barbecue and allow them to stand for 10 minutes. Place them on a cutting board and, using a large chef's knife, cut them in half down the backbone. Lay the two halves skin side up and cut those two halves into quarters. Serve with Memphis Blues Pit Beans (page 134), Creamy Coleslaw (page 157), and Memphis Blues Cornbread (page 138).

WATER SMOKER METHOD

Start the charcoal in a starter chimney. Make sure the coals are white and hot before loading. Fill the water reservoir half full. Load the charcoal into the smoker and place 2 chunks of wood on it. Or, use handfuls of wood chips placed directly on the charcoal. Put the chickens on the top rack of the smoker, breast side up. Close the lid and allow them to smoke. Keep adding hot charcoal and wood as it burns down. You may need to reload 2 times during the hour. Keep the temperature between 275–300°F (140–150°C). Cut and serve as above.

Meat

Smoked Cornish Game Hen

This is the original Memphis-inspired hen recipe. When we tried this at the Cozy Corner, we were smitten. It's quick and easy as-is, but to speed up the cooking time, split the hens along the backbone and butterfly them. **MAKES 4 SERVINGS**

four 1½ lb (750 g) Cornish game hens
¾ cup (175 mL) All-Purpose Dry Rub (page 54)
1 red onion
4 sprigs fresh sage
three 3- x 3-inch (8 x 8 cm) chunks apple wood
      OR
one 1 lb (500 g) bag of wood chips if smoking with a smoker box

GAS BARBECUE METHOD

Rub the meat with the All-Purpose Dry Rub. Make sure the hens are well coated on all sides; sprinkle some rub into each cavity. Cut the onion into quarters, wrap each quarter with a piece of sage, and stuff it into each hen. Turn on one side of the gas barbecue to create a temperature of 275–300°F (140–150°C). Put one piece of wood on the lit side of the grill. (Or, use a smoker box and refill as needed.)

Place the meat on the unlit side of the grill, breast side up. Close the lid and allow it to smoke. Once the smoke has cleared, open the lid and put in another chunk of wood. Repeat this smoking technique until all the wood is gone. The 4 hens will take approximately 1 to 1½ hours to smoke. To test for doneness, pull on a leg. If it wiggles freely and the juices run clear, it's ready. Take the meat off the barbecue and allow it to stand for 10 minutes before serving. Place the hens on a chopping board and cut lengthwise through the backbone, splitting the bird in half. Serve two halves per person. This goes great with Southwest-Style Pit Beans (page 136) and Tangy Slaw (page 159).

WATER SMOKER METHOD

Start the charcoal in a starter chimney. Make sure the coals are white and hot before loading. Fill the water reservoir half full. Load the charcoal into the smoker and place 2 chunks of wood on it. Or use handfuls of wood chips placed directly on the charcoal. Put the hens on the top rack of the smoker (breast side up), close the lid, and allow it to smoke. Keep adding hot charcoal and wood as it burns down. You may need to reload 2 times during the 1 hour. Keep the temperature between 275–300°F (140–150°C). Serve as above.

Meat

Smoked Turkey

At the restaurant, we offer whole, free-run, freshly barbecued turkeys every Thanksgiving, Christmas, and Easter. We even offer turkeys on American Thanksgiving because we have so many American expats as customers. The birds are incredibly juicy, and the breast meat has a pinkish tinge because of the smoking. MAKES 10 SERVINGS

one 12 lb (5.5 kg) turkey
1¼ cup (310 mL) All-Purpose Dry Rub (page 54)
six 3- x 3-inch (8 x 8 cm) chunks apple wood
      OR
one 2 lb (1 kg) bag of wood chips if smoking with a smoker box

GAS BARBECUE METHOD

Sprinkle the All-Purpose Dry Rub into the cavity of the turkey. Rub the outside of the turkey with the remaining rub. Turn on one side of the gas barbecue to create a temperature of 275–300°F (140–150°C). Put one piece of apple wood on the lit side of the grill. (Or use a smoker box and refill as needed.)

Place the meat on the unlit side of the grill, breast side up. Close the lid and allow it to smoke. Once the smoke has cleared, open the lid and put another chunk of wood in. Repeat this smoking technique until all the wood is gone. The turkey will take approximately 4–4½ hours to smoke. To check for doneness, pull on a leg. If it wiggles freely and the juices run clear, it's ready. Take the meat off the barbecue and let it stand for 10 minutes before carving. Serve with Cornbread and Sausage Stuffing (page 140) and Smoky Barbecue Turkey Gravy (page 128).

WATER SMOKER METHOD

Start the charcoal in a starter chimney. Make sure the coals are white and hot before loading. Fill the water reservoir half full. Load the charcoal into the smoker and place 2 chunks of wood on it. Or, use handfuls of wood chips placed directly on the charcoal. Put the turkey on the top rack of the smoker, breast side up. Close the lid and allow it to smoke. Keep adding hot charcoal and wood as it burns down. You may need to reload 2 or 3 times during the 4–4½ hours of cooking time. Keep the temperature between 275–300°F (140–150°C). Serve as above.

Meat

Smoked Leg of Lamb

We use boneless lamb shoulders in the restaurant, but using a leg is better. (It's what we use when we're entertaining at home.) Ask your butcher to debone the leg—they only come in one basic size, and are sold whole. If there are any leftovers, serve them in a sandwich or use them up in the Smoked Lamb Stew (page 174). **MAKES 8 SERVINGS**

5 lb (2.2 kg) boneless lamb leg
⅔ cup (150 mL) Brisket Rub (page 59)
five 3- x 3-inch (8 x 8 cm) chunks apple wood
               OR
one 2 lb (1 kg) bag of wood chips for smoking with a smoker box

GAS BARBECUE METHOD

Rub the meat with Brisket Rub. Make sure the leg is well coated on all sides. Turn on one side of the gas barbecue to create a temperature of 300–325°F (150–160°C). Put 2 pieces of wood on the lit side of the grill. (Or use a smoker box and refill as needed.)

Place the meat on the unlit side of the grill, fat side up. Close the lid and allow to it to smoke. Once the smoke has cleared, open the lid and put in another chunk of wood. Repeat this smoking technique until all the wood is gone. A 5 lb (2.2 kg) leg will take approximately 2½–3 hours to be pink in the middle. (Cook it longer if you prefer more well-done meat). Let it stand for 10 minutes before thinly slicing across the grain.

Serve lamb with North Carolina Mustard Sauce (page 126) and Collard Greens (page 142).

WATER SMOKER METHOD

Start the charcoal in a starter chimney. Make sure the coals are white and hot before loading. Fill the water reservoir half full. Load the charcoal into the smoker and place 2 chunks of wood on it. Or, use handfuls of wood chips placed directly on the charcoal. Put the leg on the top rack of the smoker, fat side up. Close the lid and allow it to smoke. Keep adding hot charcoal and wood as it burns down. You may need to reload 3 or 4 times during the cooking time. Keep the temperature between 300–325°F (150–160°C). Cook for 2½–3 hours. Serve as above.

Meat

Smoked Rabbit and Succotash

This recipe is not something we serve at the restaurant, but we do it at home because we love rabbit. It's almost fat free, and when smoked properly, it's very tender and succulent. Succotash is a traditional Southern dish originally made with dried beans. With the advent of excellent canned and frozen products, the recipe is now easier, quicker, and just as delicious. MAKES 4 SERVINGS

one 2½ lb (1.25 kg) fresh rabbit
½ cup (125 mL) Brisket Rub (page 59)
1 medium onion
1 medium carrot
1 stalk celery
2 cloves garlic
2 Tbsp (30 mL) canola oil
1 lb (500 g) frozen lima beans
1 lb (500 g) frozen corn kernels
1 cup (250 mL) cooked and chopped rib meat (a great time to use leftovers)
2 cups (500 mL) Memphis Blues Smoky Chicken Stock (page 168)
salt and pepper to taste
three 3- x 3-inch (8 x 8 cm) chunks apple wood
      OR
one 1 lb (500 g) bag of wood chips if smoking with a smoker box

GAS BARBECUE METHOD
Cut the rabbit into 8 pieces and rub the meat with Brisket Rub. Make sure the meat is well coated on all sides. Chop the onion, carrot, and celery. Mince the garlic. Sweat the vegetables with the canola oil in a cast-iron Dutch oven (or any

heavy flameproof casserole dish) over medium heat on your stove until the onion becomes translucent. Add the beans, corn, rib meat, and Memphis Blues Smoky Chicken Stock and continue to cook for another 10 minutes. Adjust the seasoning with salt and pepper.

Turn on one side of the gas barbecue to create a temperature of 275–300°F (140–150°C).

Put one piece of apple wood on the lit side of the grill. (Or, use a smoker box and refill as needed.)

Place the Dutch oven, uncovered, on the unlit side of the grill. Place a rack over-top and place the rabbit pieces onto it. Close the lid of the barbecue and allow the items to smoke. Once the smoke has cleared, open the lid and put in more wood. Repeat this smoking technique until all the wood is gone. The rabbit will take about 2 hours to cook through. During the last 30 minutes, wrap the rabbit in tinfoil and allow it to steam in its own juices.

When the juices run clear, they're done. Remove the meat from the barbecue and let it stand for 10 minutes. Take the Dutch oven off the barbecue and spoon the contents onto a large serving platter and unwrap the meat. Place the rabbit pieces on top of the succotash mixture. Serve with Memphis Blues Cornbread (page 138).

WATER SMOKER METHOD
Start the charcoal in a starter chimney. Make sure the coals are white and hot before loading. Fill the water reservoir half full. Load the charcoal into the smoker and place 2 chunks of wood on it. Or use handfuls of wood chips placed directly on the charcoal. Put the Dutch oven, uncovered, on the top rack of the smoker. Close the lid and allow it to smoke. Keep adding hot charcoal and wood as it burns down. You may need to reload 3 or 4 times during the cooking time. Keep the temperature between 300–325°F (150–160°C). Cook for 2½–3 hours. Serve as above.

Meat

Seafood

Seafood

Oyster Po' Boy Sandwich

A Po' Boy sandwich is a New Orleans favorite. Although there are various theories regarding the name's origin, the one we like best is that it comes from *pourboire*, which is the French expression referring to the "tip for the server." Later, it became *pour le boy*. MAKES 4 SERVINGS

2 tomatoes
¼ head iceberg lettuce
4 hoagie buns (or substitute Vietnamese crusty baguettes), cut in half
6 Tbsp (90 mL) Remoulade Sauce (page 129)
12 Deep-Fried Oysters (page 112)

Cut the tomatoes into slices and then cut the slices into halves. Shred the lettuce. Spread some of the Remoulade Sauce on both sides of the buns, then place some lettuce on the bottom half. Place 3 oysters and some tomatoes on each sandwich and top with the remaining half of the bun. You can spice it up with Brisket Rub (page 59) and Tabasco sauce if desired. Serve with Tangy Slaw (page 159) and Classic Potato Salad (page 152).

VARIATION
You can substitute Deep-Fried Catfish (page 113) for the oysters.

Pan-Fried Catfish

When we're doing a cooking demonstration in a size-limited kitchen, the absence of a deep fryer often prompts us to share this recipe (besides, it's always nice to do a seafood dish). It's quick, easy, and extremely tasty. MAKES 4 SERVINGS

¼ cup (60 mL) unsalted butter
2 Tbsp (30 mL) Seafood Rub (page 58), divided
four 6 oz (175 g) boneless, skinless catfish fillets
1 lemon

In a large, nonstick skillet, melt the butter over medium heat. Sprinkle 1 Tbsp (15 mL) of the Seafood Rub on one side of the catfish fillets; place seasoned side down in the pan. Fry the fillets for 3 to 4 minutes, flip them, and sprinkle the remaining rub onto the exposed side. Continue cooking for another 3 minutes. Remove the fillets and place them on a platter. Squeeze half of the lemon juice into the pan, and allow the drippings to mix together. Pour this juice over the fillets and serve with lemon wedges.

NOTE
This cooking method can also be used for oysters.

Smoked Mussels

When mussels are in season, we like to eat them at home. The West Coast ones are tender, with a mild flavor. This is a quick recipe that adapts well to backyard cooking. Serve them in a big bowl so everyone can share out of one pot. MAKES 4 SERVINGS

4 strips bacon
½ medium white onion
2 lb (1 kg) fresh mussels
½ cup (125 mL) dry white wine
2 tsp (10 mL) Seafood Rub (page 58)
a couple handfuls of hickory wood chips (about ½ lb/225 g)
2 green onions, chopped

Preheat one side of the barbecue to 350°F (180°C). Cut the bacon into small pieces. Sauté the bacon for 4 minutes in a cast-iron skillet over medium-high heat on the barbecue with the lid up. Chop the white onion and add to the skillet. Cook for another 5 minutes. Clean the mussels and add them to the skillet along with the wine. Sprinkle in the Seafood Rub.

Slide the skillet to the unlit side of the barbecue and load the lit side with a smoker box filled with hickory wood chips. Turn the heat to high, close the lid, and allow the mixture to smoke for 8 minutes or until all the mussels are open. Remove the mussels from the skillet and place in a large, warmed bowl (cover to keep warm). Reduce the liquid in the skillet by half over high heat. Pour the liquid over the mussels and garnish with the green onions. Place the big bowl of mussels in the middle of the table and serve with Memphis Blues Cornbread (page 138).

Barbecue Shrimp

We got this simple appetizer from an old Alabama oil man. This recipe actually has nothing to do with barbecuing. The recipe got its name from the barbecue taste that the All-Purpose Dry Rub adds. Dip bread into the butter sauce, or try tossing it with cooked noodles to create a pasta dish. MAKES 2 SERVINGS

¼ cup (60 mL) unsalted butter
10 medium-sized shrimp (31/40)
1 Tbsp (15 mL) All-Purpose Dry Rub (page 54)

On high heat, melt the butter in a nonstick frying pan. Add the shrimp and half of the All-Purpose Dry Rub. Cook for 1 minute. Turn the shrimp and sprinkle the rest of the rub into the pan. Cook for another 1½ minutes until the butter has browned and the rub has caramelized in the pan.

Remove from the heat and serve with cornbread.

NOTE

The numbers 31/40 refer to the quantity of shrimp per pound. The smaller the number, the larger the shrimp. Shrimp that are 6/8 would each be about the size of a chicken leg.

Sauces

Sauces

Memphis Blues Classic Barbecue Sauce

Most barbecue joints have a signature sauce. This is ours. We have received many requests for a bottled version, which we are planning on offering one day. Right now our focus is on keeping up with the demand in our restaurants. MAKES 1 CUP (250 ML)

2 Tbsp (30 mL) tomato paste
1 Tbsp (15 mL) dark brown or demerara sugar
1 Tbsp (15 mL) molasses
1 Tbsp (15 mL) white vinegar
1 Tbsp (15 mL) soy sauce
1 Tbsp (15 mL) honey
1 Tbsp (15 mL) ketchup
1 tsp (5 mL) yellow mustard
1 tsp (5 mL) Worcestershire sauce
1 tsp (5 mL) garlic powder
1 tsp (5 mL) onion powder
1 tsp (5 mL) Lawry's Seasoned Salt
a dash of Louisiana-style hot sauce
½ cup (125 mL) water

Combine all the ingredients in a saucepan. Whisk thoroughly or combine with a handheld blender to ensure that there are no lumps. Simmer over low heat while stirring frequently for 1 hour (this pasteurizes the sauce). Cool for at least 1 hour before transferring to an airtight container for storage. Store for up to 1 month in the refrigerator.

Tot's Coffee Barbecue Sauce

Another of Park's brother Totton's recipes. He shared it with us over a pulled pork dinner. Wow, what a revelation! MAKES ABOUT 1 CUP (250 ML)

1 medium onion
1 Tbsp (15 mL) canola oil
1 cup (250 mL) strong brewed coffee
¼ cup (60 mL) ketchup
2 Tbsp (30 mL) apple cider vinegar
1 Tbsp (15 mL) dark brown sugar
a pinch of dried chili flakes

Chop the onion into a medium dice. In a skillet, sauté the onion in the canola oil over medium heat until soft and golden. Set aside. In a saucepan, reduce the coffee to ¼ cup (60 mL). Remove from the heat, and whisk in the ketchup, vinegar, and brown sugar. Add the sautéed onion and return the saucepan to medium heat for 5 minutes. Add the chili flakes and continue cooking, stirring occasionally, for another 10 minutes.

Spicy Barbecue Sauce

When we first opened, we didn't have a hot sauce. It very soon became apparent that we needed one due to the number of requests from customers. This sauce was the result of a quick afternoon of experimentation in the kitchen. MAKES 2½ CUPS (625 ML)

2 cups (500 mL) Memphis Blues Classic Barbecue Sauce (page 122)
3 Tbsp (45 mL) white vinegar
3 Tbsp (45 mL) Louisiana-style hot sauce
2 Tbsp (30 mL) ketchup
1 Tbsp (15 mL) ground black pepper
1 tsp (5 mL) cayenne pepper
1 tsp (5 mL) chili flakes

Combine all the ingredients in a medium mixing bowl and whisk thoroughly. Serve as a condiment. It's too thick to use as a marinade, but you can use it while grilling; simply brush on the meat during the later stages of barbecuing. It keeps for up to 1 month in the refrigerator.

North Carolina Mustard Sauce

About twice a year, one of our regular customers brings in a bottle of Carolina-style mustard sauce that he picks up down in Florida. He leaves it with us, and it disappears within a few days. Recently we tried to re-create it, and this is what we came up with. Now it's a permanent fixture at all the restaurants. It's quick, easy to make, and uses a minimal number of ingredients. MAKES 2 CUPS (500 ML)

¾ cup (175 mL) yellow mustard
¾ cup (175 mL) apple cider vinegar
½ cup (125 mL) dark brown sugar
2 Tbsp (30 mL) butter
1 Tbsp (15 mL) hot sauce
1 Tbsp (15 mL) Worcestershire sauce
1 tsp (5 mL) ground black pepper

Combine all the ingredients in a medium saucepan over medium heat. Bring the liquid to a simmer and whisk to eliminate any lumps. Simmer for 20 minutes.

NOTE
Try using this sauce on the Memphis Pulled Pork Sandwich (page 74), replacing the Memphis Blues Classic Barbecue Sauce.

Honey Mustard Sauce

When we were checking out the catering operations in Memphis, we noticed that a commercial honey mustard sauce was often used instead of homemade. We developed this homemade option that we think is great (and easy to make). MAKES ABOUT ½ CUP (125 ML)

¼ cup (60 mL) liquid honey
2 Tbsp (30 mL) yellow mustard
1 tsp (5 mL) Dijon mustard
1 tsp (5 mL) mustard powder

Combine all the ingredients in a medium mixing bowl and whisk thoroughly. Serve as a condiment with barbecued lamb. This will keep for up to 2 weeks in the refrigerator.

Smoky Barbecue Turkey Gravy

This recipe is an adaptation of Park's mother's technique for making regular turkey gravy. This is the gravy we make from and for our Smoked Turkey. It's classic, and very straightforward. The big difference is that the pan juice has dry rub in it and a smoky flavor from the barbecue. MAKES 4 CUPS (1 L)

1 cup (250 mL) all-purpose white flour
a pinch of salt and pepper
a dash of dry white wine
2–3 cups (500–750 mL) chicken stock (preferably Memphis Blues Smoky
    Chicken Stock, page 168)

When your Smoked Turkey (page 100) has finished cooking, lift it out of the barbecue and into a roasting pan to rest. You will notice the pan drippings appear after half an hour; this is the foundation for your gravy. Lift your turkey onto a cutting board and set it aside for carving. Place the roasting pan onto the stovetop element on medium heat. When the juices start to bubble, whisk in the flour a little at a time until it is all used up. Continue to whisk for another 5 minutes. Add the salt and pepper, and then the white wine. Whisk until well incorporated. Add the chicken stock, a little at a time, whisking all the while. Depending on how thick you like your gravy, you can use more or less stock. Simmer the gravy for 5 minutes; it should be lump-free and glossy.

Remoulade Sauce

This French-inspired mayonnaise-based sauce has many variations. It's an integral part of the Po' Boy sandwich, but you can use it in many creative ways. We even get requests to serve it with our french fries! MAKES ABOUT 1¼ CUPS (310 ML)

1 cup (250 mL) mayonnaise
2 Tbsp (30 mL) freshly squeezed lemon juice
1 Tbsp (15 mL) Dijon mustard
½ tsp (2 mL) ground black pepper
½ tsp (2 mL) Lawry's Seasoned Salt
½ tsp (2 mL) Brisket Rub (page 59)
½ tsp (2 mL) prepared horseradish

Place all the ingredients into a bowl and whisk to combine. Keeps for up to 2 weeks in the refrigerator in an airtight container. Use on Deep-Fried Catfish (page 113), Pan-Fried Catfish (page 114), or the Oyster Po' Boy Sandwich (page 111). Or use it as a substitute for tartar sauce on the side of any fish dish.

Sides and Snacks

Sides and Snacks

Memphis Blues Pit Beans

Ideally you would make this recipe in conjunction with smoked meat. But if you don't, simply prepare your gas barbecue for indirect heat smoking (see Home Barbecue Rigs, page 38) to an interior temperature of 300°F (150°C) to cook this or any of the bean recipes in this book.
MAKES 6 SERVINGS

½ medium onion
1 Tbsp (15 mL) vegetable oil
one 28 oz (796 mL) can of beans with pork
1 cup (250 mL) Memphis Blues Classic Barbecue Sauce (page 122)
1 Tbsp (15 mL) Brisket Rub (page 59)
½ lb (250 g) Pulled Pork (page 68)

Chop the onion into a medium dice. Add the onion to a cast-iron Dutch oven (or any heavy flameproof casserole dish) and fry in the oil over medium heat until tender. Remove from the heat. Add the remaining ingredients, and mix well. Place the Dutch oven in the smoker, uncovered, over indirect heat. If you are serving with meat, place a rack on top of the Dutch oven and put the cut of meat on top of the rack. (This allows the drippings from the meat to drop into the beans as both items smoke.) Load up the wood chips and close the lid of the smoker. The beans should be done in 1½ to 3 hours, but will stand a longer smoking process if you are cooking a cut of meat that requires more time.

Southwest-Style Pit Beans

See page 134 for preparing beans in a gas barbecue by itself.

MAKES 4 SERVINGS

½ medium onion
1 Tbsp (15 mL) vegetable oil
½ lb (250 g) Beef Brisket (page 83), chopped
one 28 oz (796 mL) can pinto beans
one 14 oz (398 mL) can crushed tomatoes
1 cup (250 mL) Memphis Blues Classic Barbecue Sauce (page 122)
1 Tbsp (15 mL) Brisket Rub (page 59)
1 Tbsp (15 mL) ground cumin
a large pinch of cayenne pepper
one 2 lb (1 kg) bag of wood chips (any fruit wood or hickory)

Chop the onion into a medium dice. Add the onion to a cast-iron Dutch oven (or any heavy, flameproof casserole dish) and fry over medium heat with vegetable oil until tender. Remove from the heat and add the remaining ingredients. Mix well. Place the Dutch oven in the smoker, uncovered, over indirect heat. If you are serving with a meat, place a rack on top of the casserole dish and put the cut of meat on top of the rack. (This allows the drippings from the meat to drop into the beans as both items smoke.) Load the smoker box with wood chips and close the lid on your barbecue. The beans should be done in 1½ to 3 hours, but will stand a longer smoking process if you are cooking a cut of meat that requires more time.

To bake a flat, restaurant-style cornbread, line a 8-inch (2 L) square baking pan with parchment paper. Pour the batter into the pan and ensure it is evenly distributed. Place a small stainless steel bowl with water on the bottom of the oven. Bake in the preheated oven for 35 minutes or until the top is golden brown, rotating once during that period. Remove from the oven and let it cool at least ten minutes before serving.

Cornbread and Sausage Stuffing

This stuffing is cooked in a Dutch oven or a casserole dish, not in the turkey. We don't stuff our birds because it increases the cooking time beyond what we can do in a normal day at the restaurant. Besides, the birds are so moist and tender as is, why change a good thing?

MAKES 6 SERVINGS

1 large white onion
2 stalks celery
2 smoked sausages
3 Tbsp (45 mL) unsalted butter
2 Tbsp (30 mL) dried sage, crumbled
a pinch of salt and pepper
4 cups (1 L) crumbled Memphis Blues Cornbread (page 138)
2 cups (500 mL) Memphis Blues Smoky Chicken Stock, divided (page 168)

Preheat the oven to 350°F (180°C).

Dice the onion, celery, and sausage. In a 2-quart (2 L) cast-iron Dutch oven (or any heavy flameproof casserole dish), melt the butter over medium heat. Add the onion, celery, and sausage and sauté until the onion becomes translucent. Add the sage, salt, and pepper and continue to stir for 3 more minutes over the heat. Add the crumbled cornbread and moisten with 1 cup (250 mL) of the chicken stock. Place in the preheated oven. After 45 minutes, add the remaining chicken stock and toss. Bake for another 45 minutes. Remove from the oven once it is golden brown on top. Serve as an accompaniment to Smoked Turkey (page 100).

Barbecue Spaghetti

We saw this on a lot of menus in Memphis. It sounds a bit weird, but really, it isn't. Put this in the smoker along with any meat you're preparing. MAKES 6 SERVINGS

1 lb (500 g) dry spaghetti noodles
1 large onion
1 clove garlic
1 tsp (5 mL) vegetable oil
a pinch each of dried oregano, dried parsley, salt, pepper, and garlic powder
¼ cup (60 mL) chopped brisket
¼ cup (60 mL) Pulled Pork (page 68)
one 14 oz (398 mL) can tomato sauce
3 cups (750 mL) Memphis Blues Classic Barbecue Sauce (page 122)
2 tsp (10 mL) chili flakes

Cook the pasta al dente, according to the package directions, and set aside. Chop the onion and mince the garlic. Add the oil to a saucepan over medium heat and sauté the onion and garlic for 5 minutes. Add the oregano, parsley, salt, pepper, and garlic powder. Add the meat, stirring constantly until heated through. Stir in the tomato sauce, Memphis Blues Classic Barbecue Sauce, and the chili flakes. In a cast-iron Dutch oven (or any heavy flameproof casserole dish), combine the cooked spaghetti and the sauce mixture. Place on the top rack of the smoker beside the meat you're smoking, and smoke for 3 hours.

NOTE
Use as a starch replacement on the side of entrées, or serve à la carte.

Collard Greens

It's amazing how many people love our collard greens. They were a late addition to our menu and we special order the collards once a week all the way from California. You should be able to find them at organic markets. Otherwise, you'll have to come into the restaurant to get them! MAKES 6 SERVINGS

2 bunches fresh collard greens
1 tsp (5 mL) vegetable or canola oil
½ cup (125 mL) leftover barbecue meat (or bacon, but do not use sausage)
1 cup (250 mL) Memphis Blues Smoky Chicken Stock (page 168)
2 tsp (10 mL) garlic powder
1 tsp (5 mL) ground black pepper
1 Tbsp (15 mL) white vinegar
salt to taste

Chop the collard greens into 1 or 2 inch (2.5 or 5 cm) pieces (include the stems). Rinse well under cold water. Add the oil to a stockpot over medium heat. Add the chopped collards and the meat and sauté for 5 minutes. Add the Memphis Blues Smoky Chicken Stock and lower the heat. Simmer until the collards are partly cooked. Add the garlic powder and black pepper. Continue to simmer over low heat for 1 hour, adding the vinegar and salt during the last 10 minutes. Serve immediately, or store in the refrigerator for up to 1 week.

Barbecued Corn

This is a quick and easy side to any barbecue meal. Wait until corn is in season, and the ears are sweet and tender. **MAKES 6 SERVINGS**

6 ears of fresh sweet corn

TO SERVE
Brisket Rub (page 59)
melted butter
lime wedges

Soak the corn (still in husk) in a pot of cold water for 5 minutes. Place the corn directly over a hot barbecue flame and allow it to char, turning frequently. When the corn husks are completely charred, take the cobs off the flame, and place them in a large brown paper bag, closing it tightly. Allow the ears to steam in the paper bag for 5 minutes. Take them out and husk them. Serve with the rub, butter, and lime.

VARIATION
Husk the ears before cooking. Roast them over the barbecue flame while basting with melted butter until they are golden brown on all sides.

Memphis-Style Barbecued Nachos

This is a snack we had at a Memphis Redbirds game. We saw a kiosk selling them so we just had to try some! **MAKES 2 SERVINGS**

½ lb (250 g) plain corn chips
1 cup (250 mL) shredded Monterey Jack cheese
8 oz (200 g) Pulled Pork, warmed (page 68)
½ cup (125 mL) Memphis Blues Classic Barbecue Sauce, heated (page 122)

Preheat the oven to 375°F (190°C).

Place the corn chips on a baking sheet and cover with the grated cheese. Place the baking sheet in the preheated oven for 7 minutes or until the cheese is melted. Slide the chips off the baking sheet onto a plate and cover with the Pulled Pork. Smother with the Memphis Blues Classic Barbecue Sauce. Sprinkle with chopped cilantro and/or green onions if you like.

Sides and Snacks

Smokehouse Popcorn

This is one of those snack foods you just can't get enough of. It tastes like "More, please!" **MAKES 6 CUPS (1.5 L)**

1 Tbsp (15 mL) canola oil
1 cup (250 mL) popping corn
2 Tbsp (30 mL) unsalted butter
1 Tbsp (15 mL) All-Purpose Dry Rub (page 54)

Heat the oil over medium heat in a medium-sized, heavy-bottomed saucepan. When the oil is hot, add the popping corn, and cover with a tight fitting lid. Shake the pan directly over the heat and listen for signs of popping. When the corn starts to pop, continue to shake the contents (making sure the lid stays on tight).

When most of the popping has subsided, turn off the heat and put the pot aside, but do not take the lid off. After about 3 minutes, when the popcorn has stopped popping completely, take the lid off and turn the contents out into a large serving bowl.

Melt the butter in a small skillet or in the microwave. Drizzle the butter over the popcorn while tossing. Sprinkle the All-Purpose Dry Rub over the popcorn, continuing to toss, until evenly coated. Serve as a snack.

Dry-Rubbed Spiced Nuts

At Christmas time, we like to make homemade gifts. One of the things that our families always look forward to is a box of spiced nuts. This is our Memphis variation. MAKES 1 LB (500 G)

1 egg white
½ cup (125 mL) All-Purpose Dry Rub (page 54)
1 lb (500 g) mixed raw nuts (peanuts, hazelnuts, almonds, cashews, Brazil nuts, walnuts, pistachios, and/or pecans)

Preheat the oven to 225°F (105°C).

In a large mixing bowl, whisk the egg white until just frothy. Add the All-Purpose Dry Rub and mix thoroughly. Place the nuts into the bowl and stir to coat with the egg white mixture. Turn the nuts out onto a large, flat-bottomed roasting pan. Roast the nuts in the preheated oven for 2 hours. Remove from the oven and let them rest on the countertop for 2 hours, or until they are cooled. They will keep up to 3 weeks in an airtight container.

Salads

Salads

Classic Potato Salad

Our classic potato salad is a little bit spicy from the black pepper. It's George's recipe, and he adapted it from the one he grew up with.

MAKES ABOUT 10 SERVINGS

4 eggs
5 lb (2.2 kg) potatoes, cut into ¾-inch (2 cm) dice
2 green onions, chopped
2 stalks celery, diced
1 cup (250 mL) mayonnaise
¼ cup (60 mL) yellow mustard
1 Tbsp (15 mL) Lawry's Seasoned Salt
1 Tbsp (15 mL) ground black pepper
¼ tsp (1 mL) celery salt
a dash of hot sauce

Hard boil the eggs in boiling water for 12 minutes, then cool, peel, and coarsely chop. Add the potatoes to a large stockpot filled with boiling, salted water. Cook for 30 minutes, or until tender. Drain well and refrigerate. When the potatoes are completely cooled, combine the remaining ingredients in a large mixing bowl. Add the cooled potatoes and hard boiled eggs and combine. Taste and adjust seasonings if required before transferring to an airtight container. Store in the refrigerator for up to 4 days.

Warm Potato Salad

Anything with bacon in it is great in our books! This is a classic German-style warm potato salad. How can you go wrong? **MAKES 4 SERVINGS**

2.2 lb (1 kg) red waxy potatoes, quartered
¼ cup (60 mL) apple cider vinegar
1 Tbsp (15 mL) yellow mustard
a dash of hot sauce
2 tsp (10 mL) granulated sugar
a pinch of Brisket Rub (page 59)
a large pinch each of ground black pepper, celery seeds, and dried oregano
½ cup (125 mL) canola oil
½ cup (125 mL) cooked rib meat or bacon, chopped
1 stalk celery
1 green onion

Add the potatoes to a large stockpot filled with boiling, salted water. Cook for 25 minutes, or until tender. Drain well and set aside.

To make the vinaigrette dressing, combine the apple cider vinegar, mustard, hot sauce, sugar, Brisket Rub, black pepper, celery seeds, and oregano in a large bowl and mix well. To emulsify the dressing, slowly add the canola oil in a thin stream while whisking continuously. Set the dressing aside.

Fry the rib meat in a skillet until crispy. Add to the warm potatoes. Finely chop the celery and green onion and add to the potatoes and rib meat. Add the vinaigrette and toss. Serve while still warm.

Salads

Sweet Pickle Potato Salad

Throughout the South you see variations on this recipe. Our in-house potato salad is not this style; it's creamy with a lot of mustard tang. The most common comment we get about our potato salad from folks that come from down South is, "Why don't you put some pickle juice in your potato salad?" The answer is that neither of us likes that style very much. But hey, some people do, and that's why we've included this recipe. MAKES 4 SERVINGS

2.2 lb (1 kg) Yukon Gold potatoes, cut into ½-inch (1 cm) dice
3 cups (750 mL) Miracle Whip
¼ cup (60 mL) yellow mustard
1 Tbsp (15 mL) hot sauce
1 Tbsp (15 mL) sugar
a large pinch each of ground black pepper, celery seeds, and Lawry's Seasoned Salt
¼ cup (60 mL) sweet pickle juice
1 stalk celery
½ cup (125 mL) finely chopped sweet pickles
½ medium red onion

Add the potatoes to a large stockpot filled with boiling, salted water. Cook for 25 minutes, or until tender. Drain well and set aside to cool completely.

In a medium mixing bowl, combine the Miracle Whip, mustard, hot sauce, sugar, black pepper, celery seeds, and Lawry's Seasoned Salt. Whisk thoroughly and then add the pickle juice.

Dice the celery, pickles, and onion and add to a large bowl with the cooled potatoes. Gradually add the dressing to the bowl and toss until the salad is coated. Keep any leftover dressing in the refrigerator for up to 3 days.

Salads

Creamy Coleslaw

This salad always tastes better if you let it sit in the refrigerator overnight. MAKES 4 SERVINGS

2 tsp (10 mL) freshly squeezed lemon juice
2 tsp (10 mL) white vinegar
½ tsp (2 mL) hot sauce
¼ tsp (1 mL) Lawry's Seasoned Salt
a large pinch each of ground black pepper, mustard powder, and celery salt
¾ cup (175 mL) mayonnaise
1 cup (250 mL) packed shredded green cabbage
1 cup (250 mL) packed shredded red cabbage
½ cup (125 mL) grated carrots (or whatever other raw vegetables you like)

To make the dressing, combine the lemon juice, white vinegar, hot sauce, Lawry's Seasoned Salt, black pepper, mustard powder, and celery salt in a large mixing bowl and blend well. Add the mayonnaise and mix thoroughly. Set aside.

Combine the shredded cabbage and carrots in a large bowl. Add the dressing and mix well. Adjust the ratio of dressing to vegetables to suit your individual taste. This will keep in the refrigerator for 2–3 days. Serve on pulled pork sandwiches (pages 73 and 74), or as a side to any barbecue dinner.

Salads

Blue Cheese Slaw

The Kansas City Queens of Barbecue introduced us to this recipe when they had a book signing party in our restaurant. It goes well with lamb or brisket. **MAKES 4 SERVINGS**

¼ head green cabbage
¼ head red cabbage
1 medium carrot, peeled
1 green onion
3 oz (75 g) blue cheese
2 Tbsp (30 mL) apple cider vinegar
⅓ cup (75 mL) canola oil
1 Tbsp (15 mL) granulated sugar
1 tsp (5 mL) garlic powder
½ tsp (2 mL) celery seeds
¼ tsp (1 mL) salt
¼ tsp (1 mL) pepper

Finely shred the green and red cabbage. Grate the carrot and mince the green onion. Combine all the vegetables in a large bowl. Crumble the blue cheese overtop.

To make the dressing, whisk together the apple cider vinegar, canola oil, sugar, garlic powder, celery seeds, salt, and pepper in a medium bowl until the sugar dissolves. Pour the dressing over the shredded vegetables and mix thoroughly. Refrigerate for 1 hour before serving (this allows the flavors to meld). Serve with Beef Brisket (page 83) or Smoked Beef Ribs (page 86), or as a side to any barbecue dish.

Tangy Slaw

This slaw is an alternative to the standard vinaigrette slaw you see all over American barbecue joints. The nice thing about it is that when you pile it on a pulled pork sandwich the vinegar cuts through the richness of the meat, and the spice just adds that extra kick.

MAKES 4 SERVINGS

¼ head green cabbage
¼ head red cabbage
1 medium carrot, peeled
½ medium red onion
⅓ cup + 1 Tbsp (90 mL) apple cider vinegar
⅓ cup (75 mL) canola oil
½ cup (125 mL) granulated sugar
½ tsp (2 mL) Brisket Rub (page 59)
¼ tsp (1 mL) salt
¼ tsp (1 mL) pepper
a dash of hot sauce

Finely shred the green and red cabbage and grate the carrot. Slice onion into thin pieces. Combine all the vegetables in a large bowl.

To make the dressing, whisk together the apple cider vinegar, canola oil, sugar, Brisket Rub, salt, pepper, and hot sauce in a medium bowl until the sugar dissolves. Pour the dressing over the shredded vegetables and mix thoroughly. Refrigerate for 1 hour before serving (this allows the flavors to meld). Serve with Carolina-Style Pulled Pork Sandwiches (page 73) or as a side to any barbecue dish.

Salads

Apple Slaw

What could be better with pork than apples? Try this piled on a pulled pork sandwich . . . it's a match made in heaven! **MAKES 4 SERVINGS**

¼ head red cabbage
½ small red onion
1½ Granny Smith apples
½ cup (125 mL) mayonnaise
1½ tsp (7 mL) freshly squeezed lemon juice
1 tsp (5 mL) granulated sugar
a pinch of salt
a pinch of ground black pepper

Finely shred the cabbage and thinly slice the onion. Core the apples and slice into thin pieces. Combine the cabbage, onion, and apples in a large bowl.

To make the dressing, whisk together the mayonnaise, lemon juice, sugar, salt, and pepper in a medium bowl until the sugar dissolves. Pour the dressing over the slaw and mix thoroughly. Serve immediately as the apples tend to brown if the slaw is left to sit.

Slaw with Apples, Walnuts, and Raisins

We have often heard of barbecue sauce with raisins in it. It adds a rich sweetness. Why not try it with a slaw? This works well folks, trust US. **MAKES 4 SERVINGS**

¼ head red cabbage
1½ Granny Smith apples
¼ cup (60 mL) raisins
¼ cup (60 mL) toasted chopped walnuts
½ cup (125 mL) mayonnaise
1½ tsp (7 mL) freshly squeezed lemon juice
½ tsp (5 mL) granulated sugar
a pinch of salt
a pinch of ground black pepper

Finely shred the cabbage. Core the apples and slice into thin pieces. Combine the cabbage, apples, and raisins in a large bowl.

To make the dressing, whisk together the mayonnaise, lemon juice, sugar, salt, and pepper in a medium bowl until the sugar dissolves. Pour the dressing over the slaw and mix thoroughly. Sprinkle the toasted walnuts overtop and fold in. Serve immediately as the apples will tend to brown if the slaw is left to sit.

Salads

George's Vinaigrette

This is something we improvised during our first day—we had salads on the menu but no one had prepared any dressing! So we grabbed whatever was available on the shelves and threw it together. We still use this at our restaurants today. MAKES 1½ CUPS (375 ML)

¼ cup (60 mL) red wine vinegar
1 Tbsp (15 mL) hot sauce (we like Frank's RedHot)
1 Tbsp (15 mL) Worcestershire sauce
1 Tbsp (15 mL) soy sauce
2 tsp (10 mL) Dijon mustard
2 tsp (10 mL) garlic powder
1 tsp (5 mL) dried parsley, crumbled
1 tsp (5 mL) dried oregano, crumbled
1 tsp (5 mL) chili powder
1 tsp (5 mL) Lawry's Seasoned Salt
1 tsp (5 mL) ground black pepper
½ tsp (2 mL) celery salt
1 cup (250 mL) canola or olive oil

Combine all the ingredients, except the oil, in a medium-sized mixing bowl. Whisk until well blended. Continue whisking while slowly drizzling in the oil. Once it begins to emulsify you can add the oil in a steady stream until completely incorporated.

Croutons

This salad crouton is a Memphis twist on a standard homemade crouton. They are versatile and will taste great on any green salad. You can do these on a stovetop, but it's much easier to pop them into the oven and stir them once. **MAKES 6 CUPS (1.5 L)**

4 large hamburger buns, cubed into ¼-inch (5 mm) pieces
2 Tbsp (30 mL) canola oil
1 tsp (5 mL) dried oregano, crumbled
1 tsp (5 mL) dried parsley, crumbled
1 tsp (5 mL) garlic powder
1 tsp (5 mL) mustard powder
½ tsp (2 mL) salt
½ tsp (2 mL) ground black pepper

Preheat the oven to 350°F (180°C).

Toss all the ingredients together in a bowl. Mix well. When the bread cubes are thoroughly coated with oil and spices, turn them out onto a cookie sheet. Bake them in the preheated oven for 15–20 minutes, tossing once to evenly cook. When the croutons are evenly toasted and golden brown allow them to cool. Store for up to 2 weeks in an airtight container.

Soups and Stews

Soups and Stews

Memphis Blues Smoky Chicken Stock

We make a lot of soups, chili, collard greens, and special items that require chicken stock. We also cook a lot of chickens in the barbecue pit. What to do with all the bones? Make them into a rich, smoky stock.

MAKES 8 CUPS (2 L)

2 large onions
4 carrots
4 stalks celery
1 clove garlic
2 bay leaves
1 tsp (5 mL) whole black peppercorns
12 cups (3 L) cold water
bones and skin of 1 large Smoked Chicken (page 96)

Wash and roughly chop all the vegetables. Add all the ingredients to a large stockpot and place over high heat. As soon as it boils, reduce the heat to low. Slowly simmer for 3–4 hours, skimming the top frequently. Strain the liquid through a conical strainer into a clean container. Discard the bones and vegetables. Cover and cool the liquid overnight in the refrigerator. The following day, skim off any fat from the top and discard. Divide the liquid into smaller containers and freeze what you won't use immediately. Frozen, this stock will keep for up to 3 months.

You can use this stock in Smokehouse Chili (page 172), in Collard Greens (page 142), and in all of the soups.

Classic Smoky Chicken Vegetable Soup

This is a basic recipe, although it varies from regular chicken soup because of the smoky stock base (which makes it that much better). **MAKES 6 CUPS (1.5 L)**

1 large onion
½ red pepper
½ green pepper
2 stalks celery
2 carrots
1 Tbsp (15 mL) canola oil
1 lb (500 g) cooked chicken meat (preferably leftover barbecued meat)
4 cups (1 L) Memphis Blues Smoky Chicken Stock (page 168)
2 bay leaves
¼ tsp (1 mL) dried parsley
¼ tsp (1 mL) dried oregano
salt and ground black pepper to taste

Roughly chop all the vegetables. Heat the oil in a large stockpot and add the chopped vegetables. Sauté for 10 minutes, or until soft. Add the chicken and sauté for another 5 minutes. Stir in the Memphis Blues Smoky Chicken Stock and the dried herbs. Simmer for 1 hour. At the end of cooking, adjust the seasoning with salt and pepper.

NOTE

You may also add any dry pasta or rice when there is ten minutes left in the cooking time.

Creamy Chicken and Tomato Soup

This is a variation on a cream of chicken soup. We find that customers like creamy soups, so that's what we give 'em. **MAKES 5 CUPS (1.25 L)**

1 medium onion
1 small red pepper
1½ stalks celery
3 cloves garlic
4 oz (100 g) butter
3 Tbsp (45 mL) tomato paste
one 14 oz (398 mL) can whole crushed tomatoes
2 tsp (10 mL) dried parsley
1 tsp (5 mL) dried oregano
⅔ lb (350 g) pulled leftover Smoked Chicken meat (page 96)
4 cups (1 L) Memphis Blues Smoky Chicken Stock (page 168)
¾ cup (175 mL) whipping cream
salt to taste
1 tsp (5 mL) ground black pepper (use extra for a spicier result)

Chop the onion, red pepper, and celery into a medium dice. Mince the garlic. Melt the butter in a large stockpot over medium heat. Add the vegetables, and sauté for approximately 10 minutes, or until soft. Stir in the tomato paste, tomatoes, dried herbs, and chicken meat, ensuring that there are not bones or cartilage. Add the Memphis Blues Smoky Chicken Stock and cook over medium heat for 20 minutes. Slowly stir in the cream and simmer over low heat for 30 minutes. Add the salt and pepper.

Barbecue Brisket and Tomato Soup

Tomato and beef soup is a classic comfort food for one of those cold, wet winter days. Try this with a slice of freshly baked cornbread and a salad. A perfect meal. MAKES 5 CUPS (1.25 L)

1 medium onion
1 stalk celery
½ green pepper
½ red pepper
2 medium carrots
4 cloves garlic
1 Tbsp (15 mL) vegetable or canola oil
2 Tbsp (30 mL) tomato paste
½ lb (250 g) leftover Beef Brisket (page 83), chopped
1 Tbsp (15 mL) dried parsley
2 tsp (10 mL) dried oregano
1 tsp (5 mL) ground black pepper
4 cups (1 L) Memphis Blues Smoky Chicken Stock (page 168)
one 14 oz (398 mL) can whole tomatoes
salt to taste

Chop the onion, celery, green and red peppers, and carrots into a medium dice. Mince the garlic. Add the oil to a medium stockpot over medium heat. Add the diced vegetables and garlic and sauté for 10 minutes. Add the tomato paste and continue to cook for another 5 minutes. Add the meat, dried herbs, and pepper and mix well. Stir in the Memphis Blues Smoky Chicken Stock and the tomatoes, crushing them with your hands as you add them. Simmer for 1 hour. Add salt to taste at the end of the cooking time.

Smokehouse Chili

This chili won the consumer's choice award at the 2004 BC Place Chili Cook-off. It's the New Mexico chili powder that makes the difference. MAKES 8 CUPS (2 L)

1 large onion
2 stalks celery
1 red pepper
1 green pepper
1 Tbsp (15 mL) vegetable oil
2 lb (1 kg) leftover barbecue meat of Beef Brisket (page 83) and
        Smoked Beef Ribs (page 86)
⅔ cup (150 mL) New Mexico or Ancho chili powder
½ cup (125 mL) garlic powder
2 Tbsp (30 mL) ground cumin
2 Tbsp (30 mL) dried oregano
2 tsp (10 mL) celery salt
2 tsp (10 mL) ground black pepper
¼ tsp (1 mL) cayenne pepper
¼ tsp (1 mL) chili flakes
1 bay leaf
3 cups (750 mL) Memphis Blues Smoky Chicken Stock (page 168)
one 28 oz (796 mL) can whole tomatoes
one 28 oz (796 mL) can red kidney beans, drained
salt and pepper to taste

Chop the onion, celery, and peppers into a medium dice. Add the oil to a stockpot over medium heat. Add the vegetables and sauté until soft. Mix in the meat and seasonings. Cook for 5–10 minutes, making sure the spices don't stick to the stockpot. Stir in the Memphis Blues Smoky Chicken Stock and the tomatoes, crushing them with your hands as you add them. Add the kidney beans. Simmer over low heat, stirring often, for 2 hours. Adjust the salt and pepper to taste. Serve immediately, or cool completely and store in the refrigerator for up to 7 days in an airtight container.

Smoked Lamb Stew

Park makes a huge batch of this every St. Patrick's Day. We serve it as a special and there's rarely any left. MAKES 6 CUPS (1.5 L)

1 medium onion
2 stalks celery
2 medium carrots
4 cloves garlic
2 Tbsp (30 mL) vegetable oil
2 lb (1 kg) Smoked Leg of Lamb meat (page 102)
1 lb (500 g) potatoes
2 cups (500 mL) Memphis Blues Smoky Chicken Stock (page 168)
1 Tbsp (15 mL) Brisket Rub (page 59)
½ lb (250 g) frozen peas
salt and pepper to taste

Chop the onion, celery, and carrots into a medium dice. Mince the garlic. Heat the oil in a 2-quart (2 L) Dutch oven (or any heavy flameproof casserole dish) over medium heat. Sauté the chopped vegetables in the Dutch oven until tender. Add the garlic to the vegetables. Chop the lamb into 1-inch (2.5 cm) dice. Peel and dice the potatoes. Add the potatoes to the vegetables, stir to combine, and then add in the lamb. Continue cooking for about 10 minutes, or until the potatoes are cooked halfway through. Add the Memphis Blues Smoky Chicken Stock and bring the mixture to a simmer. Continue cooking for 15 minutes. Add the Brisket Rub.

Prepare the gas barbecue for indirect heat smoking (see Home Barbecue Rigs, page 38) at an internal temperature of 250°F (120°C). Remove the Dutch oven from the heat and with the lid off, place on the unlit side of the barbecue. Load the smoker box with wood chips, close the lid, and smoke the casserole for 3 hours. Change the smoker box 3 times for a good smoky flavor. Adjust the seasoning with salt and pepper. Add the peas when there is half an hour of cooking time left. Serve with Memphis Blues Cornbread (page 138) and Blue Cheese Slaw (page 158).

Sausage and Corn Chowder

This is our most popular soup. It is incredibly tasty, and easy to make. MAKES 8 CUPS (2 L)

1 lb (500 g) russet potatoes, peeled
1 medium onion
1 red pepper
1 green pepper
1 stalk celery
2 Tbsp (30 mL) unsalted butter
2 smoked sausages, diced
2 Tbsp (30 mL) all-purpose white flour
4 cups (1 L) Memphis Blues Smoky Chicken Stock (page 168)
1 cup (250 mL) frozen corn
one 28 oz (796 mL) can creamed corn
1 cup (250 mL) whipping cream
1 tsp (5 mL) dried parsley
1 bay leaf
salt and pepper to taste

Roughly dice all the vegetables. Melt the butter in a medium stockpot over medium heat. Add the vegetables and sweat in the butter until soft, about 10 minutes. Add the sausages and cook for another 10 minutes. Sprinkle in the flour and cook for another 5 minutes. Stir in the Memphis Blues Smoky Chicken Stock, frozen corn, creamed corn, whipping cream, and seasonings. Simmer over low heat for 1 to 2 hours, or until the potatoes are very soft. Adjust the seasoning at the end of the cooking time with salt and pepper.

Desserts

Desserts

Apple Crisp

This recipe is adaptable to other fruits or combinations of fruits. Use whatever is in season. The only rule of thumb is don't oversweeten, as the fruit has its own natural sugar. The only exception to this is when you use sour cherries and rhubarb, which require twice as much sugar.

MAKES 6 TO 8 SERVINGS

5 Granny Smith apples
¾ cups (175 mL) brown sugar
1½ tsp (7 mL) ground cinnamon
½ tsp (2 mL) ground nutmeg
1 tsp (5 mL) vanilla extract
1 Tbsp (15 mL) cornstarch

CRUMBLE TOPPING
⅔ cup (150 mL) rolled oats
⅔ cup (150 mL) chopped walnuts
¼ cup (60 mL) brown sugar
¼ cup (60 mL) unbleached all-purpose flour
½ tsp (2 mL) ground cinnamon
¼ cup (60 mL) softened, unsalted butter

Preheat oven to 375°F (190°C).

Core the apples and cut them into slices. In a large bowl, combine the ¼ cup (60 mL) brown sugar and the 1½ tsp (7 mL) of cinnamon with the nutmeg, vanilla extract, and cornstarch. Toss this mixture with the apples until the slices are well coated.

For the crumble topping, combine the oats, nuts, brown sugar, flour, and cinnamon in a bowl. Knead in the butter with your hands until the mixture becomes crumbly.

Pour the apples into an 11- x 7-inch (2 L) casserole dish. Distribute the crumble topping evenly overtop. Bake the apple crumble in the preheated oven for 45–50 minutes or until the top is brown and crispy. Allow to cool before serving with vanilla ice cream and Caramel Bourbon Sauce (page 187).

Peach Crumble Pie

Make this during peach season when local peaches are ripe and plentiful. If you insist on serving it midwinter, use frozen peaches.
MAKES 1 PIE

2 lb (1 kg) peaches, peeled and sliced
¼ cup (60 mL) brown sugar, plus extra for sprinkling
1 Tbsp (15 mL) cornstarch, plus extra for sprinkling
½ tsp (2 mL) ground cinnamon, plus extra for sprinkling
one 9-inch (23 cm) unbaked pie shell

CRUMBLE TOPPING
½ cup (125 mL) rolled oats
½ cup (125 mL) chopped walnuts or pecans
¼ cup (60 mL) unbleached all-purpose flour
¼ cup (60 mL) brown sugar
½ tsp (2 mL) ground cinnamon
¼ cup (60 mL) softened, unsalted butter
pinch salt

Preheat the oven to 425°F (220°C).

To make the peach filling, mix together the peaches, brown sugar, cornstarch, and cinnamon in a large bowl, making sure the peaches are coated. Place the peach filling into the pie shell and sprinkle a little sugar, cinnamon, and cornstarch overtop.

To make the crumble topping, combine the rolled oats, nuts, flour, brown sugar, and cinnamon together in a bowl. Cut the butter into small pieces and knead it into the crumble mixture with your hands until the mixture becomes crumbly. Evenly sprinkle the crumble overtop of the pie and bake in the preheated oven for 50–60 minutes.

When the crumble comes out of the oven, cool it on a cooling rack for several hours. Once cooled, serve with vanilla ice cream and a good drizzle of Caramel Bourbon Sauce (page 187).

Desserts

Sweet Potato Pie

We get lots of calls for sweet potato pie. We serve it from time to time as a special feature. It is a real old-time favorite in the Deep South. For those unfamiliar, its taste and texture are a lot like good old Canadian pumpkin pie. MAKES 1 PIE

4 large sweet potatoes or yams
½ cup (125 mL) unsalted butter
½ cup (125 mL) whole milk
½ cup (125 mL) brown sugar
2 large eggs
1 tsp (5 mL) vanilla extract
a large pinch of ground cinnamon
a large pinch of ground nutmeg
one 9-inch (23 cm) unbaked pie shell

Preheat the oven to 350°F (180°C).

Bake the sweet potatoes in the preheated oven for 1 hour or until very tender. Cool, peel, and mash the potatoes. Use an electric mixer to smooth the mashed potatoes. Add the remaining ingredients. Mix again until smooth.

Pour the batter into the unbaked pie shell. Place the pie into the middle of the preheated oven and bake for 1 hour. Allow the pie to cool before serving with whipped cream or vanilla ice cream.

NOTE
At Memphis Blues, we prefer to use yams as they are sweeter and lend a more orange color to the pie.

Bourbon Pecan Pie

This is one of our favorites. The bourbon just adds a special kick to an otherwise classic Southern dessert. MAKES 1 PIE

1 cup (250 mL) chopped pecans
3 Tbsp (45 mL) bourbon
3 Tbsp (45 mL) unsalted butter, melted
3 large eggs
½ cup (125 mL) brown sugar
1 cup (250 mL) corn syrup
1 tsp (5 mL) vanilla extract
¼ tsp (1 mL) salt
one 9-inch (23 cm) unbaked pie shell

Preheat the oven to 375°F (190°C).

Soak the pecans in the bourbon and set aside for 30 minutes. Using an electric mixer, beat together the butter, eggs, and brown sugar until fluffy. Blend in corn syrup, vanilla extract, and salt. Sprinkle the pecans into the pie shell and pour the wet mixture overtop. Bake for 45–50 minutes. Allow to cool before serving with vanilla ice cream and Caramel Bourbon Sauce (page 187).

Caramel Bourbon Sauce

This dessert garnish is so popular we almost have to keep it under lock and key at the restaurants. MAKES 1 CUP (250 ML)

1 cup (250 mL) granulated sugar
¼ cup (60 mL) water
¾ cup (175 mL) whipping cream
¼ cup (60 mL) Jim Beam bourbon

Pour the sugar and water into a large saucepan and gently mix until just combined. (Use a spatula to clean off the edges of the saucepan to prevent burning.) Place over high heat until the mixture turns a golden red/brown color (do not stir). Slowly add one-third of the cream (about ¼ cup/60 mL) while whisking thoroughly. When it is a smooth consistency and starts to bubble up again, add the rest of the cream, still whisking. The trick is to maintain the high temperature while whisking in the cream gradually. (It will tend to boil so be careful.)

Remove the saucepan from the heat before whisking in the bourbon (watch out for flare-ups!). Put the saucepan back over medium heat and stir constantly for 2 minutes. (This allows the alcohol to cook off.) Cool completely. Store in the refrigerator for up to 2 weeks. Use as an accompaniment for the Apple Crisp (page 180) or Bourbon Pecan Pie (page 186).

Drinks

Drinks

Simple Sugar Syrup

The syrup recipe given here is a standard sugar syrup recipe used in bars all over North America. We use it in cocktails and in other sweetened drinks. MAKES 2 CUPS (500 ML)

1 cup (250 mL) granulated sugar
1 cup (250 mL) water

In a heavy saucepan, combine the sugar and water. Place over medium-low heat, whisking continuously, for 15 minutes, or until the sugar completely dissolves. Allow it to cool and store it in an airtight container. It will keep well for weeks in the fridge.

Fresh Lemonade

Fresh lemonade is essential to any Southern menu. It's refreshing and keeps well. We sell lots. MAKES 8 CUPS (2 L)

2 cups (500 mL) freshly squeezed lemon juice
2 cups (500 mL) Simple Sugar Syrup (page 192)
4 cups (1 L) cold water

Combine all the ingredients in a large jug and mix well.

VARIATION
For an alcoholic version, see Lynchburg Lemonade (page 195).

Lynchburg Lemonade

In order to call this Lynchburg Lemonade you must use Tennessee whiskey. (But if you use Kentucky bourbon, it's still delicious.)

MAKES 1 SERVING

1½ oz (45 mL) Jack Daniel's Tennessee whiskey
1 cup (250 mL) Fresh Lemonade (page 193)
1 slice lemon

Fill a tall glass full of ice cubes. Add the whiskey and top with the lemonade. Garnish with the lemon slice.

Bourbon Peach Cobbler

We serve this drink as a summer special at our Commercial Drive location (nicknamed cocktail central). It's a refreshing way to take the heat off a sultry midsummer day. **MAKES 1 SERVING**

1½ oz (45 mL) bourbon whiskey
1 oz (30 mL) peach liqueur
3 or 4 ice cubes
1 oz (30 mL) Southern Comfort
soda water
1 peach slice

In a cocktail shaker, combine all the ingredients, except the soda water, and shake well for 30 seconds. Pour into a tall cocktail glass. Top with soda water and garnish with a slice of fresh or canned peach.

Mint Julep

At catered events, this cocktail is always the most popular. It's trendy, refreshing, and summery. **MAKES 1 SERVING**

1 oz (30 mL) freshly squeezed lemon juice
5 sprigs fresh mint
1 Tbsp (15 mL) granulated sugar
1½ oz (45 mL) bourbon whiskey
3 or 4 ice cubes
soda water

Add the lemon juice, mint, and sugar to a rocks glass. Using the back of a spoon, crush the mint into the sugar until the sugar is nearly dissolved. Add the bourbon and ice. Top with soda water.

Drinks

John Collins

This is a classic summer drink. Most Canadians are used to gin or vodka, but we challenge you to try this one. It's delicious!

MAKES 1 SERVING

1½ oz (45 mL) bourbon
1 oz (30 mL) freshly squeezed lemon juice
1 Tbsp (15 mL) superfine sugar
crushed ice
3 oz (90 mL) soda water
1 cocktail cherry
1 orange slice

In a tall glass, combine the bourbon, lemon juice, and sugar. Mix well with a spoon. Fill the glass with crushed ice and top with soda water. Garnish with the cherry and orange slice.

Bourbon Sour

The good old whiskey sour is a standby in Canadian bars, but use bourbon instead of rye. Very refreshing. MAKES 1 SERVING

1½ oz (45 mL) bourbon
1 Tbsp (15 mL) egg white
½ tsp (2 mL) superfine sugar
juice of ½ a lemon
3 or 4 ice cubes
1 cocktail cherry
1 orange slice

In a cocktail shaker, combine the bourbon, egg white, sugar, lemon juice, and ice cubes. Place the lid on the shaker and shake vigorously for 15 seconds. Strain into a short glass and garnish with the cherry and orange slice.

Index